AF408521

This text was originally published in India on the year of 2023.
The edits and layout of this version are Copyright © 2023
by I J N

This publication has no affiliation with the original Author or publication company.

Crafting of Clear Thinking

I J N

India
2023

CONTENTS

INTRODUCTION

In October 2004, a European media mogul invited me to Munich for what they described as an informal exchange of intellectuals. While I hadn't considered myself an intellectual myself - having studied business rather than literature - my two literary novels must have qualified me for such an invite.

Nassim Nicholas Taleb was sitting at the table. At that time, he was an obscure Wall Street trader with a passion for philosophy who I met as an expert on English and Scottish Enlightenment philosophy, especially that of David Hume. Evidently I had been mistaken for someone else. Shocked at my mistake, but still trying to maintain composure, I flashed a tentative smile around the room in hopes that silence would serve as proof of my philosophical abilities. At that moment, Taleb pulled over an available chair and patted its seat; inviting me to sit. I did so. After briefly discussing Hume, our conversation quickly moved onto Wall Street. We marveled at the systematic errors in decision making by CEOs and business leaders - ourselves included! We discussed why unexpected events seem more probable with hindsight, while discussing why investors refuse to sell shares once their value drops below acquisition cost.

After the event, Taleb sent me pages from his manuscript; an incredible gem that I reviewed and commented upon in part; this became part of The Black Swan, his international best-seller that catapulted him into intellectual all-star status. Meanwhile, my appetite was whetted; I began devouring books written by cognitive and social scientists on topics such as heuristics and biases as well as increasing email conversations with researchers as well as visiting their labs - by 2009 I had realized that alongside being a novelist I had become a student of social cognitive psychology as well.

Experts define cognitive errors as systematic deviations from logic - optimal, rational thought and behavior that deviates from an ideal state. By "systematic," I mean these deviations from optimal thought aren't just occasional misjudgements or judgment errors but are rather repeated missteps, obstacles to logic we come up against time after time across generations and centuries. Overestimating our knowledge is more prevalent than underestimating it! For instance.
Underestimate is what most often happens. Additionally, fear of losing something motivates us far more than the prospect of making similar gains; when in the presence of other people we often adjust our behavior to match theirs; anecdotes tend to obscure statistical distribution (base rate) behind an event, making errors pile up like dirty laundry in one corner while leaving other corners relatively clean (i.e. in what has come to be known as the "overconfidence corner") instead.

I began making a list of cognitive errors to avoid gambling with what wealth I had amassed throughout my literary career and to safeguard against unnecessary risks with that wealth, with no intention of publishing the list in future publications. I originally intended this list for use by myself only. Some of the thinking errors have been around for centuries while others may only recently been recognized. Some also come with two or three names attached; I chose those most widely utilized. Soon I discovered that creating such a list could not only aid my investing decisions, but also business and personal matters. Once complete, creating this list helped me feel calmer and clearer-headed. I began to recognize my errors earlier, enabling me to correct course before any lasting damage was caused. Additionally, for the first time ever in my life I could identify when others may also be falling victim to these systematic mistakes. With my list, I could now resist their pull - and even gain an upper hand in my dealings. Now I had categories, terms, and explanations with which to ward off irrationality's threat - like Benjamin Franklin flying his kite during thunderstorms; thunder and lightning haven't become less frequent, powerful, or loud - yet are becoming less troubling; something which resonated deeply within myself when faced with my own irrationality now.

Friends quickly took note of my compendium, showing interest and prompting a weekly newspaper column in Germany, Holland and Switzerland as well as numerous presentations (mostly to medical doctors, investors, board members, CEOs and government officials) until this book came about.

Keep these three points in mind as you explore these pages: first, this list is incomplete - there may be new errors discovered. Second, most errors seem connected and should come as no surprise; after all, all brain regions are connected via neural projections that travel throughout our bodies.
Thirdly, my expertise lies primarily as a novelist and entrepreneur rather than social scientist; as such I do not possess my own laboratory for conducting cognitive error experiments or employing researchers to monitor behavioral errors. So in writing this book I thought of myself more like a translator whose role it is to interpret and synthesize what I've read and learned so others may comprehend it more readily. For that I have immense gratitude towards those researchers who have, over decades, revealed behavioral and cognitive errors; their research is indebtedness pays dividends that makes this book possible, for which they deserve my gratitude as I thank them hugely.

This book is not a how-to book; there won't be seven steps to an error-free life here. Cognitive errors have become too ingrained for us to ever completely rid ourselves of them, nor should this even be our goal; some cognitive errors may even be essential in leading a happy life and should therefore remain there; though this book may not hold the key to happiness, at the very least it acts as protection from excessive self-induced unhappiness.

My goal is simple: if we could learn to recognize and avoid major blunders in thinking in our personal, professional, and political lives, perhaps prosperity would increase dramatically. All it requires is less irrationality - none of this extra cunning or new gadgetry needed here.

Why It Is Important to Visit Cemeteries

Rick can find rock stars everywhere he looks: television screens, magazine pages, concert programmes and online fan sites are flooded with images and songs of them; their presence cannot be avoided at the mall or gym - there are hundreds of them! Rick believes there must be something wrong with him since these stars appear so frequently and reliably in his life. Rick was inspired by stories of many guitar heroes to start his own band and begin performing live music, but chances are he won't make it big like them; like so many before him he will most likely join thousands of failed musicians who reside in a graveyard of failed musicians which houses 10,000 times more musicians than the stage does yet no journalist cares to cover failures other than fallen superstars - rendering this cemetery invisible from outsiders.

At work and in everyday life, success often seems more visible than failure, causing us to overestimate the probability of succeeding. Just like Rick, outsiders often fall for this illusion and misjudge its likelihood. Rick is just another victim of "Survivorship Bias".

Behind every successful author there may be 100 other writers whose books will never sell; another 100 haven't found publishers; and still another 100 whose unfinished manuscripts linger unread in drawers. Behind each one of these books are 100 people who dream of one day publishing a book - but you only hear of successful writers (many of whom self-publish), failing to appreciate their incredible odds for literary success. Photographers, entrepreneurs, artists, athletes, architects, Nobel Prize winners, television presenters and beauty queens must also dig themselves out from under the survivorship bias in order to combat its effect. No one else will do it for you! To overcome survivor bias yourself.

Survival bias also arises in financial decisions: consider that your friend opens a start-up. As one of their potential investors, you see an incredible opportunity here: it could become the next Google or Amazon. However, reality check: in most cases such ventures fail outright or close within months or years of starting; second likely outcomes include either bankruptcy or just plain survival - either option being equally likely.
Outcome: the likelihood is that any business formed will go bankrupt within three years; of those that survive that long, most never reach beyond ten employees. So should you never risk your hard-earned money in any venture? Not necessarily; just remember that survivorship bias distorts the probability of success like cut glass.

Take, for instance, the Dow Jones Industrial Average Index: it comprises only successful businesses; failed and small firms do not enter the stock market despite representing most business ventures. Thus a stock index does not accurately depict an economy and similarly the press does not report on all musicians equally; similarly the abundance of books and coaches dealing with success should make you wary as these unsuccessful individuals don't write books or give lectures about their failures.

Survival bias can be particularly dangerous when one becomes part of a winning team. Even when success arises out of chance, similarities with other winners might tempt us to identify these similarities as key success factors; yet a visit to graveyards of failed individuals and companies will reveal many similar traits among its tenants that contributed to yours!

If enough scientists investigate a phenomenon, some studies will produce statistically significant findings through sheer coincidence - for instance the correlation between red wine consumption and high life expectancy. Such "false" studies quickly gain popularity and attention - unlike studies with less exciting yet correct findings that remain hidden away in academia's back pages.

Survival bias refers to people overestimating their chances of success. One way of combatting it is visiting the graves of once-promising projects, investments and careers regularly; although this might be uncomfortable at times it should help clear your mind and provide some much-needed closure.
See also Self-Serving Bias (ch. 45); Beginner's Luck (ch. 49); Base Rate Neglect (ch. 28); Induction (ch. 31); Neglect of Probability (ch. 26); Illusion of Skill (ch. 94) & Intention-To-Treat Errors (ch. 98).

DOES HARVARD MAKE YOU SMARTER?

Nassim Taleb decided to do something about his stubborn extra pounds by taking up various sports activities, but soon became disenchanted with them all - from jogging and tennis players to bodybuilders and bodybuilders. Swimming appealed more due to their well-built and streamlined bodies - so he signed up at his local pool and started training twice weekly at that pool.

Shortly thereafter, he realized his fall into illusion: professional swimmers don't achieve perfect bodies by training endlessly; rather, their physiques determine whether they become great swimmers - not vice versa. Female models advertising cosmetics also create the impression that using them makes one beautiful; but this belief stems from consumers mistakenly thinking the products make women model-like; rather it is simply their natural attractiveness that attracts buyers; just like professional swimmers' bodies are chosen because of it and not vice versa.

When we confuse selection factors with results, we become vulnerable to what Taleb calls "the swimmer's body illusion." Without it, half of advertising campaigns would fail without it working at all - yet this bias goes much deeper than just an obsession for having defined cheekbones and chests. Harvard is widely considered one of the premier universities, with many successful people studying there. Does this indicate that Harvard is an outstanding educational establishment? No. Perhaps Harvard just attracts bright students. Experienced this phenomenon first hand at University of St Gallen in Switzerland, one of the ten top business schools in Europe; yet I found the lessons (25 years ago!) disappointing and many graduates successful despite this; possibly due to climate or cafeteria food - though more likely due to rigorous selection processes.

MBA schools lure candidates with impressive statistics about future earnings potential. Many prospective students fall for this approach to demonstrate that tuition fees pay for themselves over time, yet many fall victim to it themselves. I'm not suggesting schools manipulate statistics; still their statements should not be taken at face value because individuals who pursue an MBA differ significantly from those who don't, with differences in income stemming from many sources other than just the MBA itself - another instance of the "swimmer's body illusion." So if further study is on your agenda, do it for reasons other than just making more money later.

When I ask happy people about the key to their contentment, I frequently hear responses such as 'You need to look at things as half full instead of half empty' - suggesting they do not recognize that they were born happy and instead see opportunities in everything around them. Studies conducted at Harvard by Dan Gilbert reveal that cheerfulness is largely an enduring personality trait that remains unchanged throughout life. Social scientists Lykken and Tellegen have made this point clear; trying to be happier is just as futile as trying to grow taller. Accordingly, swimmer's body illusion is also self-illusion; when optimists write self-help books further propagating this delusion. At this point, it's crucial that we avoid giving too much consideration to advice from self-help authors. Unfortunately, their suggestions don't tend to help billions of people - yet, as most unhappy people don't publish books about their failures, this reality remains hidden from view.

Conclusion: it's best to exercise caution when being encouraged to strive for certain things - be they abs of steel, immaculate looks, a higher income, long life span or happiness - since these might lead to swimmer's body illusion. Before making a leap of faith and diving in head first, look in the mirror first - be honest with what you see there!

See also Halo Effect (Ch. 38); Outcome Bias (Ch. 20); Self-Selection Bias (Ch. 47)and Alternative Blindness (Ch.71) for further insight.

WHY YOU SEE SHAPES IN THE CLOUDS

Clustering Illusion
In 1957, Swedish opera singer Friedrich Jorgensen purchased a tape player to record his vocals. While listening back, strange noises and whispers that seemed supernatural appeared. A few years later he recorded birdsong; during one recording session, his deceased mother's voice could be heard whispering in the background: 'Fried, my little Fried... Can you hear me... Mammy is calling.' After this encounter, Jorgensen dedicated himself to communicating with those departed through tape recordings.

Diane Duyser from Florida experienced something similar when, while biting into a piece of toast and returning it to her plate, she noticed an image of Mary within it. At that instant she stopped eating and put the divine message away for safe keeping (minus one bite). Later that November 2004, Diane auctioned off this still fairly well preserved snack via eBay and was rewarded with $28,000!

In 1978, a woman in New Mexico experienced something similar; her tortilla's blackened spots resembled Jesus' face. The media picked up on this story, drawing thousands to New Mexico to view Jesus in burrito form. Two years earlier - 1976 - Viking Spacecraft photographed rock formation that looked similar. It made headlines around the globe; known as 'Face on Mars'.

Have You Seen Faces in the Clouds, Animal Outlines in Rocks or Hidden Messages in Diffuse Signals Before? Probably. This is perfectly normal: our brain seeks patterns and rules, and when none exist it simply creates them itself! Diffuse signals such as background noise on tape make it easier for us to spot "hidden messages". Twenty-five years after discovering the "Face on Mars", Mars Global Surveyor returned clear images showing rock formations with human faces dissolving into mere rock scree.

These whimsical examples may make the clustering illusion appear harmless; but it is far from harmless.

Consider financial markets, which produce massive volumes of information every second. Unbeknownst to him, my friend delighted in explaining how he had discovered an anomaly among all the data: multiplying the percentage change of Dow Jones by the percentage change in oil price would yield the gold price move within two days' time - meaning if share prices and oil climb or fall simultaneously, gold will follow suit and rise the next day. His theory worked well for several weeks until he began investing with ever larger sums and eventually lost all his savings - sensing an artificial pattern where none existed!

Psychology professor Thomas Gilovich interviewed hundreds of people for an answer as to whether this sequence was random or planned, with most rejecting an arbitrary explanation as they believed some law governed its order. According to Gilovich's dice physics model it's actually quite possible for four consecutive rolls to reveal one number; yet many struggle accepting that such events occur by chance alone.

During WWII, German bombers attacked London using V1 rockets - a type of self-navigating drone - as one form of ammunition. Each attack involved carefully plotting impact sites onto maps to terrorise Londoners; many thought they had identified patterns and developed theories regarding which parts of London were safest; however, postwar statistical analyses demonstrated that distribution was completely random due to V1 rocket's inaccuracy as its navigation system was so inaccurate.

Conclusion: when it comes to pattern recognition, we tend to overreact. Regain your scepticism; if you think you have discovered a pattern, first assume it could have happened by chance and consider statistical analysis before reaching a decision. Likewise if crispy parts of your pancake resemble Jesus' face in any way whatsoever, ask yourself why He hasn't shown himself here in Times Square or CNN instead!
See also Illusion of Control (ch. 17); Coincidence (ch. 24); False Causality (ch. 37).

Social Proof Imagine this: you're on your way to a concert when at an intersection you see a group of people looking upward. Without thinking twice, you too look upward - without even realising why - unconsciously following suit. Why? Social Proof. During an exceptional soloist's performance at a concert hall, someone starts clapping, prompting others in the room to join in clapping as well; you join in too for no other reason than social proof. After the performance ends you head off to collect your coat check where people queue ahead of you leave coins even though service included within ticket price but even so... after which, when going to coat check to retrieve it yourself, you observe people leaving coins on plates instead despite officially being included within ticket price as tipping is encouraged in practice by many other concertgoers leaving a tip as well for social proof!

Social proof or the "herd instinct," dictates that individuals feel validated when their behaviors conform with those of other individuals. Simply stated, the more people who support or adopt an idea or behaviour we perceive it to be truer; similarly, when more individuals show it than not. Although obviously ridiculous, this logic holds.

Social proof is the driving force behind financial bubbles and stock market panic. It manifests in fashion, management techniques, hobbies, religion and diets; sometimes leading to such dramatic consequences as when sects commit mass suicide.

Solomon Asch conducted an intriguing experiment during the 1950s which demonstrated how peer pressure can change reality. Subjects were shown a line drawn on paper and three identical, short, medium, and long lines which correspond to it on different parts of their bodies - all marked "1, 2," for shortness; longer than original line in length and same as original one respectively. He or she must choose which of three lines correspond to the original one, unsurprising given how straightforward the task is. Once five people enter, all actors unfamiliar to him give incorrect responses by answering with "number 1," even though it is clear that number three should be indicated instead. When it is back up to him again he often answers incorrectly to match what other people responded with - in about one third of cases giving wrong answers as well.
Why do we act this way? In the past, following others was often seen as the best strategy for survival. Imagine traveling around Serengeti together with some hunters-gatherers 50,000 years ago when suddenly all of them scattered and bolted without warning? How would you respond then? Would you have stood there, confused and questioning whether what you saw was really a lion or simply something harmless that could make for great protein-rich meals? No! Instead, you'd likely have taken off in pursuit of your friends. Later on when you were safe from attack, you might have taken time to consider who your "lion" had really been. Anyone acting differently from their peers - which I'm sure there were - was likely eliminated

from our gene pool; we are the descendants of those who copied what their peers did. We humans are hardwired with this pattern of social proof; therefore we use it even when there's no survival advantage to it; which is most of the time. There are, however, instances when social proof can be advantageous: for instance when dining out in a foreign city without knowing any good restaurants nearby and hungry - selecting one where locals frequent might make more sense and copy their behavior instead of your own.

Comedy and talk shows utilize social proof by inserting canned laughter at strategic spots to encourage viewers to laugh along. Perhaps one of the most remarkable and disquieting examples is Joseph Goebbels' speech before an enormous audience in 1943 (watch it yourself on YouTube). When war worsened for Germany, Goebbels demanded from attendees: 'Do you want total war? If necessary, do you support radical war as opposed to anything we can even imagine today?" His demand caused a thunderous applause; had individual attendees been asked individually they likely wouldn't have accepted this insane proposition!

Advertising makes the most of our penchant for social proof; this approach works well when we face uncertainty (such as choosing among various car makes, cleaning products and beauty products with no clear advantages or disadvantages) and when people who appear 'like us' appear.

Be skeptical whenever a company claims their product is superior because it's popular - this argument makes little sense if selling more units does not indicate superiority! And remember W. Somerset Maugham's words of wisdom: 'Even if 50 million people say something foolish, it remains foolish.'
See also: Groupthink (ch. 25); Social Loafing (ch. 33); In-Group Out-Group Bias (ch. 79) and False-Consensus Effect (ch. 77) for further reference.

WHY YOU SHOULD FORGET THE PAST

Sunk Cost Fallacy
After an hour-and-a-half of watching an awful film, I quietly asked my wife: 'Come on, let's go home.' To which she responded with: 'No way; we won't throw away $30.' At that point I protested: 'That's no reason to stay - that's simply deformation professionnelle at work here - which should not play any part in our decision to stay or leave!' Naturally enough I eventually gave in and sank back down into my seat

I found myself sitting in a marketing meeting the next day where an advertising campaign that had been running for four months but failed to meet even one goal was under discussion. While I advocated scrapping it, our advertising manager objected: 'But we've already invested so much money into it; stopping now would mean all our money had been for nothing'- another victim of the sunk cost fallacy.

One of my friends suffered for years in a difficult relationship. His girlfriend would repeatedly cheat, repentantly asking forgiveness each time. Nonetheless, my friend kept investing energy into their romance because it felt wrong to throw away what had already been invested; an example of the "sunk cost fallacy."

The sunk cost fallacy is particularly hazardous when we have invested an extensive amount of time, money, energy or emotion into something. Our investment can become the basis of continuing despite obvious reasons to stop; the more time and resources invested means the greater our sunk costs are; hence our need to keep going even if something seems impossible or hopeless. The more invested in something the stronger is our urge to carry on;

Investors frequently fall victim to the sunk cost fallacy. Trading decisions may be driven solely by acquisition prices; invoking this argument as justification is simply not rational; what matters more than price should be the future performance (and other alternatives available to invest) of each stock or portfolio of investments - ironically the more money is lost, the longer investors will tend to stick by it!
Consistency is our raison d'etre; when something breaks from this pattern of thought and action, we find the contradictions abhorrent and opt to cancel midway through rather than admit to changing our minds at some point in the project's lifetime. Delaying painful realisation by continuing with meaningless projects keeps up appearances for longer.

Concorde was an iconic example of government deficit spending. Both Britain and France knew full well that supersonic aircraft business wouldn't work, yet still invested enormous sums to save face. Abandoning it would have meant conceding defeat; hence its name, "Concorde effect." It leads to costly and even disastrous errors of judgement; Americans extended involvement in Vietnam War because of this phenomenon: they thought: 'We have sacrificed so much; giving up now would be wrong.'

Are You Thinking "We Have Come This Far?." "I Have Read So Much Of This Book Already..." If any of these statements apply to you, they indicate the sunk cost fallacy is at work in your mind.

Of course, investing to finalise something may have its own advantages; just be wary of doing it solely to justify non-recoverable investments. Rational decision-making demands you forgetting about past costs; ultimately only future costs and benefits matter when making rational choices.

See also: It-Will-Get-Worse-Before-It-Gets-Better Fallacy (ch. 12); Inability to Close Doors (ch. 68); Endowment Effect (ch. 23); Effort Justification (ch. 60); Loss Aversion (ch. 32) and Outcome Bias (ch. 20) as other cognitive biases that lead to inappropriate decisions.

Reciprocity

Recently, you may have encountered followers of the Hare Krishna sect floating about in their bright saffron-colored robes while you raced through airports or train stations on your journey to reach your destination. Perhaps one member gave you a small flower and smiled warmly as they gave it. Like most people, chances are you took the flower just to avoid being rude. Refusing might have drawn out an explanation such as, 'Take it; this is our gift to you.' When trying to dispose of the bloom in a trashcan nearby, there were already multiple arrangements there; when looking elsewhere for its disposal you found that there were already multiple piles. As your bad conscience began niggling at you more strongly another disciple of Krishna would approach asking for donations; many airports eventually banned this sect due to this successful pitch;

Robert Cialdini can explain the success of these campaigns with his research into reciprocity. He found that people find it very hard to be indebted to another individual.

Many non-governmental organisations and philanthropic organisations employ similar strategies: first give, then take. Recently, I received an envelope containing postcards featuring idyllic landscapes from a conservation organisation; their accompanying letter assured me they should be kept as gifts, regardless of my decision to donate money. While I understood their tactics well enough, it required considerable willpower and discipline on my part to put them away without taking advantage of them!

Unfortunately, this form of gentle blackmail - sometimes also referred to as corruption - is common. A supplier of screws might invite potential customers to join him at an exciting sports game; come ordering time a month later, their desire not to be in debt is so strong that the buyer agrees and places an order through this new acquaintance.

Reciprocity is an ancient principle found among all species with fluctuating food supplies. Imagine you're a hunter-gatherer who, one day, manages to kill a deer and must divide it among your group members; doing this ensures you will benefit from other's spoils if your haul was less impressive; they serve as refrigerators.
Reciprocity is an invaluable survival strategy and form of risk management, without which humans - as well as many species of animal life - would soon perish. Reciprocity lies at the core of cooperation among people unrelated to one another and is integral for economic growth and wealth creation - without it there would be no global economy at all! That is the benefit of reciprocity.

However, reciprocity also brings with it its dark side: retaliation. Revenge breeds counter-revenge until full-scale war ensues. Jesus preached that we should break this cycle by turning the other cheek - although this proves difficult as reciprocity pulls even when stakes are far less high.

Years ago, we were invited by a couple we had only known casually; they were nice enough but far from entertaining. Unfortunately, it turned out exactly as imagined: their dinner party was beyond boring; yet we felt obliged to invite them again several months later out of reciprocity; only weeks later did another invitation from them arrive...I often wonder how many other dinner parties have endured in order to maintain reciprocity?

Similar to when approaching in the supermarket, my best advice would be to decline their offer of wine, cheese or olives unless you want your fridge filled up with stuff you don't even enjoy.

See also Framing (ch. 42); Incentive Super-Response Tendency (ch. 18); Liking Bias (ch. 22) and Motivation Crowding (ch. 56) to learn more.

WATCH OUT FOR "THE SPECIAL CASE'

WHEN CONFIRMATION BIES BEWARE! (Part 1).

Gil is on a diet to shed pounds. Every morning he steps on the scales, checking for progress against his selected plan and celebrating each loss or gain as evidence that it's working or writing it off as normal fluctuations. For months on end, however, his weight remains steady while Gil lives under an illusion that the diet works despite it not actually doing anything - an example of confirmation bias at play in its harmless form.

Confirmation bias is at the core of most misconceptions. It refers to our tendency to interpret new information so it fits within existing theories, beliefs and convictions - effectively filtering out any evidence which contradicts existing views (known as disconfirming evidence) which might challenge them (which Aldous Huxley famously wrote about as "Facts do not cease existing if ignored") but this dangerous tendency persists among humans - super-investor Warren Buffett states it best: 'Humans excel at interpreting all new information so their prior conclusions remain intact'

Confirmation bias is alive and well in business today. For instance, consider this: an executive team decides on a new strategy, celebrating any sign it might work well - while any indications that indicate otherwise remain unseen or are quickly dismissed as exceptions or special cases - until disconfirming evidence becomes invisible to them altogether.

What can you do? Be wary when the word 'exception' surfaces; often this indicates disconfirming evidence is present. Take a cue from Charles Darwin: from early in his youth he set out systematically to counter confirmation bias by taking very seriously any observations that conflicted with his theory, recording them immediately as soon as they appeared - knowing full well how easily our brains "forget" disconfirming evidence after some time has passed - taking note of each contradiction as soon as he saw it appear and actively searching out contradictions based on his assessment of its correctness - more so the more he looked actively he looked out.

This experiment highlights how challenging it can be to question our own theories. A professor presented his students with the number sequence 2-4-6.
Students were challenged by their professor to determine the underlying rule written on a sheet of paper by providing numbers in sequence that either fit the rule or did not, with replies such as 'fits the rule' or 'does not fit the rule' from him. While students could guess numerous numbers at random from 8-14 for instance (most suggested 8 and received the response: 'Fits the rule.' To be certain they tried 10, 12 and 14 and were told every time by

Professor that these did fit). Many concluded: 'The rule is adding two to each number;' only to have Professor disagree with them by saying this is not in fact what the rule is;

One savvy student tried an unconventional approach. He tested out the number -2, to which his professor responded by saying that it did not fit the rule, before suggesting seven as fitting more closely than its predecessor -2. When this proved fruitless, the student experimented further by trying -24, 9, 43.... When no more counterexamples could be found he stated 'The rule is: each successive number must exceed its predecessor.' Turning over his sheet of paper revealed this exact rule!

What distinguished the resourceful student from his peers? While most students sought only to confirm their theories, he actively searched for evidence disproving them. You might think: 'Good for him but not big deal for the others.' However, falling prey to confirmation bias is no petty intellectual offense - as revealed in subsequent chapters it can affect our daily lives drastically.

See also: mes disponibilite Bias (ch. 11); The Feature-Positive Effect (ch. 95); Coincidence (ch. 24); Forer Effect (ch. 64) and Illusion of Attention (ch. 88).

MURDER YOUR DARLINGS

CONFIRMATION BIAS PART 2

In our previous chapter, we explored one of the core fallacies - confirmation bias. Human beings must form beliefs about life, economics, investments, careers and much more - from our worldview to politics to economics to art - that must then be supported with evidence to support these assumptions. Whether one goes through life believing that people are intrinsically good or bad they will find evidence supporting either view. Philanthropists and misanthropes alike filter disconfirming evidence while favoring those that uphold their respective worldview by prioritising those that reinforce their views with do-gooders or dictators who promote them.

Astrologers and economists operate with similar strategies: making predictions so vague that any event could substantiate them: 'in the coming weeks you will experience sadness,' or 'medium term pressure on the dollar will increase' are both vague enough for any event to bear out these predictions; depreciation measures against gold, yen, pesos wheat residential property prices in Manhattan Manhattan Manhattan hotdog prices

Religion and philosophical beliefs serve as fertile ground for confirmation bias to flourish. Here in its soft sponginess it thrives wild and free - for instance worshipers always find evidence for God's existence even though He rarely shows himself overtly - except to illiterates living in remote mountain villages; never showing himself to mass audiences like Frankfurt or New York. Counterarguments against his existence are dismissed outright by believers, showing just how strong this force really is.

Business journalists may be particularly susceptible to confirmation bias. When creating theories, business journalists frequently come up with easy explanations with few pieces of 'evidence' supporting it and then move on quickly with writing their story - for instance: Google is so successful because its culture promotes creativity. Once this idea has been written down, journalists usually corroborate this claim with examples of other prosperous companies which cultivate creativity while rarely seeking disconfirming evidence such as struggling businesses with an emphasis on creativity or flourishing firms that lack any creativity whatsoever - both groups would make great stories!
Journalists tend to overlook multiple members of a clan; any attempt by them to highlight just one could derail the entire plotline of their article.

Self-help and get-rich-quick books are another example of one-sided storytelling. Their savvy authors amass evidence supporting even seemingly ridiculous theories, like 'meditation is key to happiness.' Any reader searching for disconfirming evidence would find no such evidence here: nowhere are there examples of people leading fulfilled lives without meditation or those despite practicing it still feeling sadness.

Internet sites provide an especially fertile ground for confirmation bias. When browsing news sites and blogs to stay informed, we often end up selecting pages that reinforce our existing values - whether liberal, conservative, or somewhere in between. In addition, many websites now tailor content specifically to individual interests or browsing history, rendering new or differing opinions unwelcome altogether and leading us down paths that reaffirm existing convictions by surrounding ourselves with like-minded communities that reinforce those same convictions - further reinforcing confirmation biases and reinforcing our convictions further reinforcing them further reinforcing them and further strengthening convictions which reinforces confirmation bias.

Arthur Quiller-Couch had an enduring mantra: 'Kill Your Darlings.' This advice for writers struggling to cut cherished but redundant sentences resonated widely beyond literary critics and hackers; his advice resonates with us all suffering from confirmation bias. To combat it, try writing down all your beliefs - worldview, investments, marriage, healthcare, diet or career strategies - and set out looking for disconfirming evidence against each. Cutting beliefs which feel like old friends is difficult work but vitally necessary!

See Also: Introspection Illusion (ch. 67); Salience Effect (ch. 83); Cognitive Dissonance (ch. 50); Forer Effect (ch. 64) and News Illusion (ch. 99) for more details.

TAKE NOTE OF AUTHORITIES' WORDS

Authority Bias

In Genesis 1, God tells us what happens if we disobey one of his authority figures: expulsion from paradise. Unfortunately, less divine figures (political pundits, scientists, doctors, CEOs, economists, government heads, sports commentators and stock market gurus) would like us to believe this as well.

Psychologist Stanley Milgram conducted an experiment that vividly illustrated authority bias. His subjects were instructed to administer increasing electrical shocks to an individual seated behind glass pane. Starting with 15 volts, they were instructed to gradually increase to 30V, 45V and then finally the maximum dose of 450V - although no electrical current actually flowed - Milgram used an actor as his victim; unfortunately those administering shocks were unaware. Results were shocking: as the person in the other room wailed in pain and the subject administering shock wanted to stop, their professor would encourage them to continue because 'this experiment depends on it.' Most continued electrocution; over half went up to full voltage out of sheer obedience.

Over the past decade, airlines have also become aware of the perils associated with authority bias. In earlier days, captains ruled supreme; their commands could never be challenged and any co-pilot who suspected an oversight may never have dared speak out about it.
Since this behavior was discovered, nearly every airline has implemented Crew Resource Management (CRM). CRM coaches pilots and their crews to discuss any reservations openly and quickly; in other words: deprogramming authority bias. CRM has contributed more to flight safety in recent decades than technical advancement.

Many companies lack foresight. Businesses with dominant CEOs are particularly at risk, where employees may keep their less favorable opinions to themselves - likely to the detriment of the company as a whole.

Authorities seek recognition and are always finding new ways to consolidate their status. Doctors and researchers often wear white coats. Bank directors wear suits and ties; bank directors don ties while crown-wearing kings use rank badges from the military; members of the military often sport rank badges too! Today more symbols and props are used as markers of expertise such as talk show appearances or magazine covers, book tours or Wikipedia entries; with authority evolving much like fashion does and society taking notice accordingly.

Conclusion: Before making any major decision, always think carefully about which authorities might be exerting an impactful influence over your reasoning process and try your best to challenge those in power if necessary.

Robert Cialdini recounts in his book Influence the tale of two brothers named Sid and Harry who ran a clothing store during 1930s America; Sid was responsible for sales while Harry headed up tailoring services. Sid would become hard of hearing whenever customers who stood before his mirror were overwhelmingly pleased with their suits, prompting him to ask Harry: 'Harry, how much for this suit?' Harry would then look up from his cutting table and respond quickly by shouting back that for this beautiful cotton suit it cost $42. Sid would act confused and pretend he hadn't understood. Harry would exclaim: 'Forty-two dollars!' Sid then turned around and reported back: 'He says $22.' By this time, his customer would have quickly put money on the table before quickly leaving with their suit before poor Sid realized his error.

Know this experiment from your school days? : Fill two buckets - one with lukewarm and the other with icy water - then immerse your right hand for one minute into each. Switch hands back over, placing both of them back into lukewarm water simultaneously - what have you noticed? Right hand finds it hot while left hand finds it cools just fine!

These stories illustrate the contrast effect: when presented with something ugly, cheap, or small we tend to judge it as more beautiful or expensive; conversely we find absolute judgement difficult.

Contrast effect is a pervasive illusion: when purchasing leather seats for your new car, compared with its $60,000 price tag, $3,000 seems inconsequential compared to its overall cost. All industries offering upgrade options take advantage of this misleading perception to lure consumers in and sell upgrades.

Contrast effect can also play a vital role elsewhere: experiments show that people will walk an extra ten minutes if it will save $10 on food, yet would never consider walking back for saving $10 on an expensive suit; an irrational move since 10 minutes equal 10 dollars regardless. Therefore, walking back should always be undertaken or simply don't happen at all.

Without the contrast effect, discount businesses would cease to exist entirely.
An untenable position exists when product prices drop from $100 to $70 in an instant; starting price should not play any role here. An investor once told me a stock was great value because it had fallen 50 per cent below peak price; I responded in kind by shaking my head: stock prices never have low or high points - all that matters is whether they move upward or downward from there on out.

If we encounter contrasts, our brains respond much like birds to a gunshot: we flutter out and move quickly. Unfortunately, though, our tendency is not to recognize gradual changes as they occur: an illusionist could make your watch vanish without you even realizing because when pressed against one part of your body by pressing against another part you don't notice when his lighter touch on your wrist removes your Rolex watch from it; similarly we fail to observe how our money disappears through inflation which slowly robs it value away whereas imposed as taxes (which in essence it really is) we would react much more strongly against such taxes (which in reality it basically amounts to).

Contrast is a dangerous force: A beautiful woman marries a more average man; but, because her parents were disreputable individuals, he seems like an extraordinary figure to her.

One final thought: with all the advertisements featuring supermodels, we now view beautiful people as only moderately desirable. When searching for love, never go out with supermodel friends as people will perceive you less attractive than you really are if you go alone or bring two ugly friends along instead.

See also:Availability Bias (ch. 11); Endowment Effect (ch. 23); Halo Effect (ch. 38); Social Comparison Bias (ch. 72); Regression to Mean (ch. 19); Scarcity Error (ch. 27); Framing (ch. 42)

Saying something such as, 'Smoking isn't that harmful if my grandfather managed to survive by smoking three packs a day and living to be over 100' or: "Manhattan is really safe; my friend lives right in the Village without locking his door even during vacation - his apartment has never been broken into!" can be used to try to prove a point, yet they actually prove nothing at all; in doing so we succumb to availability bias.

Are more English words that start with K, or more with it as their third letter,? Answer: Over two times as many English words feature K in third position than start with it; although many believe the latter to be more numerous. People mistakenly believe otherwise due to being more likely to recall words beginning with a K more quickly; therefore these are easier for our memories.

The availability bias states: our minds tend to create an image of reality based on examples we find most easily in our memories, even though these events don't actually occur more frequently because they can be easily imagined.

Due to availability bias, we often navigate life with an inaccurate risk map in mind. Because of this bias, we tend to overestimate our risks of plane crashes, car accidents or murder while underestimating those from less spectacular causes such as diabetes or stomach cancer. Bomb attacks are less frequent than we believe while depression rates can be much higher - this bias leads us to give too much weight to spectacular outcomes while downgrading quiet or invisible ones more readily than we should; our brains favor showy outcomes more readily than mundane ones - this leads us thinking in dramatic rather than quantitative ways!

Doctors frequently succumb to availability bias: they use their usual treatments in all possible cases, even though more suitable ones might exist but remain hidden in their memory banks. Consultants, too, often fall prey to this phenomenon - rather than dismiss a completely unfamiliar case by saying: 'I really don't know' they try their best not to act out on intuition but take action instead.
Instead of finding out exactly what they should tell you, people often fall back on one of their tried-and-tested approaches, no matter if it is ideal or not.

Repetition can create a long-term imprint in our minds; something repeated often enough becomes part of the collective consciousness, even if its content is false; just ask Nazi leaders how often they repeated "The Jewish Question", before people started believing it was an important issue! All it takes to start believing these concepts is saying the words UFO, life energy or karma enough times before people take note and believe them!

The availability bias has become a well-established feature on corporate boards worldwide. Board members tend to focus their discussions on what management has submitted - usually quarterly figures - instead of addressing more important matters, such as competition moves, employee motivation issues or changes in customer behavior that might impact them directly. They don't tend to discuss things outside the agenda. People tend to favor easily accessible information - whether economic data or recipes - when making decisions; making their choices on this basis rather than more pertinent but harder-to-access data could prove disastrous for their decisions. Example: we have known for 10 years that the so-called Black-Scholes formula for pricing derivative financial products doesn't work, yet due to a lack of viable solutions, we continue using an inappropriate tool. It would be like being in an unfamiliar city without a map but then finding one for home from somewhere and using that instead - preferring incorrect information over no information at all - thus leading banks to incur billions in losses due to availability bias.

Frank Sinatra famously sang: 'Oh my heart is beating wildly/All because of you/When I'm not near the one I love/I still love her." This is an example of availability bias - to combat it effectively we need the input from others with different experiences and expertise than ourselves in order to overcome its effects.
See also Ambiguity Aversion (ch. 80); Illusion of Attention (ch. 88); Association Bias (ch. 48); Feature-Positive Effect (ch. 95); Confirmation Bias (ch. 7-8); Contrast Effect (ch. 10); Neglect of Probability (ch. 26) for more on this subject.

WHY "NO PAIN, NO GAIN" SHOULD SOUND ALARM BELLS

THE "IT WILL GET WORSE BEFORE IT GETS BETTER FALLACY"

Once, while vacationing in Corsica, I became sick. The symptoms were unfamiliar and pain was increasing by the day. So I sought medical assistance at a nearby clinic. A young doctor began inspecting me carefully - prodding my stomach, gripping shoulders and knees tightly and poking each vertebra for signs of problems. His examination seemed strange to me but I persevered until his notebook came out with antibiotics written on it: 'Take one tablet three times daily until your symptoms subside. Take your antibiotics until the symptoms improve before considering medication as treatment!' When done I made my way back to my hotel room with prescription.

Pain worsened over the next three days - just as predicted by my doctor. Though he must have known what was wrong with me, when the pain didn't subside after three days I called him again to ask what to do about it and was advised by him to increase dosage to five times daily for "it may hurt for awhile more". After another two agonizing days passed I decided to call an international air ambulance where the Swiss doctor diagnosed appendicitis immediately before operating immediately on me, asking afterward, "why did you wait so long?".

"Everything went exactly according to what the doctor predicted, so I trusted his advice."

"Oh no! You fell for the fallacy that says things will only worsen before they improve." Your Corsican doctor was likely unaware of this; likely just another tourist trap during peak season.'

Take another example: a CEO finds themselves frustrated, with sales in the toilet, salespeople not motivated and marketing campaigns fizzling out completely. In desperation, he hires a consultant at $5,000 a day whose assessment includes findings that include your sales department lacking vision and your brand not being clearly positioned - I can fix both for you but it may take longer before improvements happen - most likely sales will decrease further before things improve' The CEO hires this consultant; one year later sales decline once more before progress occurs, as emphasized by this consultant; repeatedly during these consultations they stress how closely progress is connected with company progress as measured against his findings on analyses made available by his findings on this day by this man whose analysis.
As sales continue their downward spiral in the third year, the CEO decides to fire the consultant.

The It-Will-Get-Worse-Before-It-Gets-Better Fallacy is simply an excuse, an example of confirmation bias. If the problem continues to worsen as predicted, confirmation bias confirms itself whereas if unexpected improvement occurs unexpectedly then customer is pleased and the expert can take credit for his skillset; either way he wins.

Imagine yourself as president of a country, without the know-how to manage it effectively. What would your first move be? Perhaps forecasting "difficult years", asking citizens to tighten their belts and promising improvement after this delicate stage of "cleansing", "purification", and "restructuring", leaving open how long and severe this period might last?

Christianity stands as the ultimate testament of this strategy's effectiveness: its believers believe that before experiencing heaven on Earth, the world must first be destroyed through disasters like floods, fires and deaths - these all form part of God's bigger plan - any worsening of conditions as an indication that their prophecy was fulfilled; any improvements seen as God's blessing.

Conclusion: When someone says, 'It will get worse before it gets better,' this should raise alarm bells. However, beware: situations do exist where things first deteriorate before improving over time; for instance a career change often includes loss of pay while restructuring of a business can take time as well. But in all of these instances we can see relatively quickly whether measures taken are working; milestones provide clear indicators. Focus instead on these rather than seeking relief through magical solutions.

See also Action Bias (ch. 43); Sunk Cost Fallacy (ch. 5); Regression to the Mean (ch. 19) for further explanation.

Life can be confusing. Consider an invisible Martian following you around with an equally invisible notebook to document everything you do, think and dream. Your life would read like this: 'Drank coffee with two sugars'; "Stepped on a thumbtack and swore like a sailor", 'dreamed that I kissed my neighbor", 'booked vacation to Maldives but now nearly out of money", or 'found hair poking out from under my ear - plucked it immediately". These would all be entries in your journal that chronicle what is going on each day - the entries would keep coming. People enjoy weaving the pieces of their lives into a coherent tale, forming stories from scattered details that we call meaning and identity respectively. Max Frisch, an esteemed Swiss novelist once noted: 'We try on stories like clothes.

As humans, we use narrative to make sense of global history, condensing disparate events into a coherent storyline. Through this lens we come to comprehend certain issues; such as why the Treaty of Versailles contributed to World War Two or why Alan Greenspan's loose monetary policy caused Lehman Brothers' collapse. Understandings can vary; here, we refer to understandings as understanding, but these things cannot be comprehended in their original state - we create meaning from them later. Stories are highly subjective entities. They often distort reality and filter out anything that doesn't fit, yet we are powerless without them. Why this is still unclear. What we know for certain is that humans first used stories as ways of explaining the world before becoming scientific; thus making mythology older than philosophy and giving rise to story bias.

Story bias runs rampant in media reports. To give one example: when a car drives over a bridge and it suddenly collapses, what do we read the next day? A tale about its unfortunate driver; where they came from and where they were headed; we read his biography (born somewhere, raised elsewhere, earning their living somewhere else); if he survives and can give interviews we get details on exactly what he felt when the bridge collapsed - but none of these tales explain its cause - just skip past them all
Consideration should also be given to the bridge itself: where was its weak point, whether fatigue caused it and whether damage was done; was an appropriate design used and were there similar bridges similar to this one. While all these questions are valid ones, their answers don't make for engaging stories; we like stories over abstract details. Therefore, entertaining side stories are prioritized over relevant facts (which, on the upside, would mean we would only ever read non-fiction books!)

Here are two tales by English novelist E. M. Forster for you to consider; which would you remember best? A) "The King Died and Queen Died of Grief.' B) 'The King Died and Queen Died from Grief." Most will likely recall story B more easily as its two deaths don't just take place successively but are linked emotionally; A is more factual while B has deeper significance - information theory suggests we should remember A more easily due to it being shorter but our brains don't work that way!

Advertisers have learned to exploit this fact as well, by creating compelling narratives around products rather than just their benefits. Google illustrated this technique perfectly in their 2010 Super Bowl commercial called 'Google Parisian Love' on YouTube - take a look for yourself here.

Reducing reality into meaningful stories distorts reality and affects our decisions; to correct this distortion there is one remedy. Pick apart these narratives. Ask yourself: what are they trying to hide? Visit a library and spend half a day reading old newspapers; you will see that events that now appear connected weren't at the time; additionally try viewing your life story out of context: dig through old journals and notes to discover that life has not followed a straight path leading directly towards today; instead it has been an unplanned, unpredictable series of experiences and events - something we will explore further in chapter 5.

As soon as you hear a tale, consider who it came from and its intentions; what has been left unsaid; what details might have been left out that might even more pertinent than what's presented, for example when discussing financial crises or war. One problem with stories: they give us an false sense of security.
Understanding inevitably drives us to take greater risks and tread cautiously across uncharted waters.

See False Causality (ch.37); 'Because' Justification (ch.52); Personification (ch.87); Hindsight Bias (ch. 14); Fundamental Attribution Error (ch. 36); Conjunction Fallacy (ch. 41); Falsification of History (ch.78); Cherry Picking (ch.96) and News Illusion (ch. 99) as additional issues to consider.

Hindsight Bias Recently, I came across my great-uncle's diaries. In 1932 he moved from a Swiss village to Paris in search of filmmaking opportunities and made this entry just two months after France was invaded: 'Everyone believes that German forces will leave by December, with England falling quickly afterward; then our lives in Paris can finally resume under Germany.' Unfortunately this occupation lasted four years.

Today's history books present German occupation of France as part of an organized military strategy; therefore it seems likely in retrospect. Unfortunately, we have fallen prey to hindsight bias.

Now consider this example from 2007: economic experts projected bright prospects for the following years, yet within one year financial markets imploded. When asked to explain this crisis by reporters, experts listed its causes: Greenspan's monetary expansion; lax mortgage validation standards; corrupt rating agencies; low capital requirements and so forth - in hindsight these explanations seem increasingly obvious.

Hindsight bias is one of the most pervasive fallacies. We could refer to it as the 'I told you so' phenomenon: when looking backwards everything becomes evident and predictable. If a CEO finds success through sheer hard work and sheer luck, their perception of its probability is often much higher than it really was. Following Ronald Reagan's triumphant election victory over Jimmy Carter in 1980, commentators predicted his appointment despite its closeness up until days before final voting day. Today's business journalists appear convinced of Google's eventual dominance even though such predictions would have caused laughter had they been made back in 1998. One startling fact: today it seems heart-wrenchingly plausible that one shot fired in Sarajevo in 1914 would lead to 30 years of conflict and cost 50 million lives - something every school child is taught in school - but back then nobody would have dreamed of.
Escalation would have seemed too absurd.

What makes hindsight bias so dangerous? Simply, it leads us to believe we are better predictors than we actually are and causes arrogant overconfidence in our knowledge, leading us to take too much risk with global issues as well as local ones: "Have you heard? Sylvia and Chris have separated. It was always going wrong since they're such different personalities - or just so similar - or maybe they spent too much time together or barely saw each other".

Overcoming hindsight bias can be difficult. Studies have demonstrated that even people aware of it often fall for it, so I sincerely regret wasting your time reading this chapter.

If you have made it this far, I offer one final tip based on personal rather than professional experience: keep a journal. Record any predictions related to political changes, your career development, weight issues or stock markets. After some time has passed, review these predictions with actual developments in order to assess any discrepancies. Be surprised at how bad your forecasting skills are! Don't just read history textbooks either - don't rely solely on retrospective theories from retrospect! Diaries, oral histories, and historical documents from that period offer invaluable information that eludes even experts! Those who can't do without news should read newspapers from five, ten, or twenty years ago - this will provide an even deeper sense of how unpredictable our world can be. Looking back may provide temporary comfort; but for deeper revelations into how everything works we will benefit more by looking forward.

See also: Fallacy of the Single Cause (ch. 97); Falsification of History (ch. 78); Story Bias (ch. 13); Forecast Illusion (ch. 40); Outcome Bias (ch. 20) and Self-Serving Bias (ch. 45) as additional perspectives to consider when overestimating knowledge and ability.

WHY DO WE CONSTANTLY OVERESTIMATE OUR KNOWLEDGE AND ABILITIES?

Johann Sebastian Bach was not just one-hit wonder; his work is numerous and will be discussed further at the end of this chapter. For now, here's a simple assignment for you to try estimating how many concertos he composed; pick a range from 100-500 ideally with 98% accurate estimates and only 2-2% variances between estimates.

How confident should we be in our own knowledge? Psychologists Howard Raiffa and Marc Alpert posed this same question to hundreds of individuals they interviewed through interviews and focus groups. They asked participants to estimate total egg production in the U.S. or estimate the number of physicians and surgeons listed in Boston Yellow Pages directory or estimate foreign automobile imports into U.S. or even estimate toll collections of Panama Canal in millions of dollars. Subjects were asked to select any range they desired with an aim of not being incorrect more than 2% of the time, yet in reality were off by 40%! Researchers labeled this amazing phenomenon overconfidence.

Overconfidence applies to forecasting in terms of stock market performance over a year or profits over three years, as well as forecasts of our knowledge and ability to predict. People often underestimate both our knowledge and ability to forecast, and also our confidence that individual estimates are correct or incorrect; rather it measures what people know versus how confident they feel they are in making predictions. It may surprise some that experts suffer even more than laypeople from overconfidence; when asked to predict oil prices five years from now an economics professor may give his prediction with greater conviction than his counterpart would do; yet when asked to predict oil prices five years out, even more confidently than their counterpart would give his forecast!

Overconfidence extends beyond economics: surveys reveal that 84% of Frenchmen estimate themselves to be above-average lovers; without overconfidence effects, that figure should have been exactly 50%; statistical median means 50% should rank higher and 50% lower respectively. Another survey shows 93% believe they are above-average lovers despite this overconfidence effect.
U.S. students surveyed estimated themselves as "above average" drivers, and 68% of University of Nebraska faculty rated themselves in the top 25% for teaching ability. Entrepreneurs and those wishing to marry also perceived themselves to be superior: they believed they could beat odds. Without overconfidence existing, entrepreneurial activity would likely decrease dramatically; for instance every restaurateur hopes their restaurant will become the next Michelin-star establishment but many fail within three years due to poor returns on investments that remain consistently below zero.

Hardly any major projects ever complete on time and at less cost than forecast. Notable examples include the Airbus A400M, Sydney Opera House and Boston's Big Dig. To understand why, two forces come into play simultaneously: overconfidence is one factor; secondly, those directly interested in the project often have incentives to understate costs: consultants, contractors and suppliers all seek more business. Builders feel encouraged by optimistic figures while politicians gain more support through these activities - we will discuss strategic misrepresentation (Chapter 89).

What makes overconfidence so pervasive and its effect so troubling is its inexorability: it does not respond to incentives, being an instinctual trait rather than driven by incentives; neither is its counterpart, "underconfidence", present. Not surprisingly for some readers: male overconfidence tends to be more prominent while women don't tend to exaggerate their knowledge and abilities nearly as much; furthermore optimists aren't alone when it comes to overestimating themselves - even self-proclaimed pessimists still overrate themselves albeit less extreme.

Conclusion: Remember to remain aware that it is easy for us to overestimate our knowledge. Be wary of predictions from experts; in all plans, favor the pessimistic scenario as this gives you a chance of accurately judging situations more realistically.

Back to our question at hand: Johann Sebastian Bach left behind 1127 works that have survived until today, though many may have been lost over time. For further reading see: Illusion of Skill (ch. 94); Forecast Illusion (ch. 40) and Strategic Misrepresentation. (Ch. 89); Incentive Super-Response Tendency (Ch. 18); Self-Serving Bias (Ch. 45).

DO NOT TAKE NEWS ANCHORS SERIOUSLY

After being awarded the Nobel Prize for Physics in 1918, Max Planck went on a nationwide lecture tour through Germany to present new quantum mechanics theories. Wherever he went he delivered the same lecture. Over time, his chauffeur became familiar with his speech: 'Professor Planck must find repeating himself monotonous; let me do it for you in Munich? Sit front row wearing my chauffeur's cap and wear my chauffeur cap as that would give us both some variety!' Planck was delighted with this idea, so the driver held an evening lecture on quantum mechanics before an elite audience. When one of Munich's physics professors stood up with a question for him, his driver became surprised: 'Never would I have expected someone from such an advanced city as Munich would pose such a simple query! My chauffeur will happily provide an answer.'

Charlie Munger, one of the world's premier investors (from whom I have taken this story), identified two types of knowledge. Real knowledge can be seen among those who have spent significant time and effort understanding a topic; chauffeur knowledge refers to knowledge from people who know how to put on a show with impressive voices or stunning hair styles; however, their words come off like they're reading from script.

Unfortunately, it has become more challenging than ever to distinguish true knowledge from chauffeur knowledge. News anchors provide a good example of this dichotomy; everyone knows these actors are simply performing roles - yet I continue to be amazed at the respect these polished script readers command in addition to moderating panels on topics they barely comprehend themselves.

Journalists present more challenges. Some journalists possess true expertise; these veteran reporters usually specialize in one field for years. These reporters make an effort to comprehend a subject's complexities, then explain it effectively through long articles that detail cases and exceptions. Most journalists, however, resemble chauffeurs: writing one-sided texts quickly using Google searches without doing much research for compensation; their texts tend to be one-sided, short and one-dimensional in content. These individuals tend to display little knowledge, while exuding an air of superiority in tone.

Business can often exhibit superficiality. As companies become larger, CEOs are expected to possess "star quality". Unfortunately, dedication, solemnity, and reliability often go undervalued at the top. Sometimes shareholders and journalists mistakenly believe that showmanship will produce better results which is certainly not true.

Warren Buffett, Munger's business partner, has come up with an excellent solution: his "circle of competence". What falls within this circle can be understood intuitively while what lies outside it may only partially make sense. Munger advises people to remain within what he refers to as their circle of competence: understanding what you understand and don't. Size doesn't matter as long as they know where their perimeters lie.' Munger emphasizes this point. To find success in any endeavor, one must understand their own aptitudes. If playing against people with greater aptitudes than themselves is to your detriment, and you don't, it will likely end in loss - that much can be guaranteed. Therefore, to find an edge and to remain within one's circle of competence is of utmost importance.'

Conclusion: Be on the lookout for chauffeur knowledge. Do not mistake company spokespersons, ringmasters, newscasters, schmoozers or verbiage vendors as experts with true knowledge. One clear indicator: true experts know when their expertise ends and when it begins again; true experts also recognise when something falls outside their circle of expertise, and keep quiet or speak freely to indicate such knowledge gaps; chauffeurs rarely do this with regards to themselves!

See also Authority Bias (ch. 9); Domain Dependence (ch. 76); Twaddle Tendency (ch. 57) for further explorations.

Every night around nine o'clock, at approximately nine thirty, an individual in a red hat stands in a square and begins wildly waving their cap around. After five minutes he disappears and one day later when approached by policeman, this individual replied he was keeping away giraffes but none could be seen here so must be doing an effective job at it!' To this the policeman replied "Well then I must be doing well then!"

One day when my friend with a broken leg was housebound and asked me to buy him lottery tickets for him, I went into town, checked some boxes, wrote his name on it and paid. However, as soon as I gave it him he objected: 'Why did you do that? I wanted to fill it out myself; these numbers won't win me anything!"

"Do you really think picking numbers will have any bearing on the draw?" I inquired. His face blankly met my gaze.
Casino players often throw the dice as hard as possible if they need a high number, and more gingerly when hoping for low ones - an absurd practice much like football fans hoping they can influence a game by gesticulating in front of a television set. Unfortunately they share this illusion with others who also seek to influence world affairs by sending out positive vibes or "karma."

Jenkins and Ward discovered in 1965 the illusion of control, the tendency to believe we can affect something over which we have no influence, through an experiment using two switches and a light. By flicking switches they were able to influence when and whether the light came on at random; subjects still believed they could influence its brightness by flicking switches.

Consider this example: an American researcher conducted tests to investigate acoustic sensitivity to pain by placing people in sound booths and gradually increasing volume until subjects signalled him to stop. His two rooms (A and B) were identical except that B featured a red panic button on its wall.
The button was only meant as an illusion of control; however, its presence gave participants the sense that they could shape their situation and thus enable them to tolerate significantly greater noise levels. If you have ever read Aleksandr Solzhenitsyn, Primo Levi or Viktor Frankl, this finding should come as no surprise; their books describe how even minor influences on destiny encouraged prison inmates not to give up hope.

Crossing streets in Los Angeles can be tricky, but at the touch of a button we can stop traffic - or can we? The purpose of the button is to make us believe we have some control over traffic lights, so that we may endure waiting longer without becoming impatient or losing patience with waiting for it to change more patiently. Similar tricks are employed when it comes to elevator 'door-open/close' buttons: many aren't even connected to an electrical panel! Similar measures have also been implemented into open plan offices: for some it may always be too hot, while for others too cold. Clever technicians create the illusion of control by installing fake temperature dials; this reduces energy bills - and complaints. Such strategies have come to be known as placebo buttons and they're being employed everywhere from elevators and offices to stores with checkout counters.

Central bankers and government officials utilize placebo buttons expertly. An example would be the federal funds rate - an extremely short-term, overnight interest rate. Though this rate doesn't affect long-term interest rates (which depend on supply and demand and are therefore crucial in investment decisions), its every change elicits strong reactions in the stock market. No one understands why overnight interest rates have such an effect on markets, but everyone thinks they do and so it happens. Statements by the Federal Reserve Chairman can have the same impact: markets move even though his words provide little of actual tangible benefit for real economy; they merely create sound waves. Yet we allow economic heads to continue playing with illusory dials. A real wake-up call would come if all parties involved understood that global economy is ultimately out of our hands and cannot be managed effectively.

Are You Confident That Everything Is Under Control? Probably Less Than You Think
See also Coincidence (ch. 24); Neglect of Probability (ch. 26); Forecast Illusion (ch. 40); Illusion of Skill (ch. 94); Clustering Illusion (ch. 3); Introspection Illusion (ch. 67) in this chapter.

Super-Response Tendency

French colonial rulers in Hanoi in the 19th century enacted a law to control an infestation of rats: for every dead one brought in to authorities, its catchers would receive a reward. Many rats were destroyed through this initiative but also many more bred specifically for it.

Archaeologists who discovered the Dead Sea scrolls in 1947 set a finder's fee per parchment; instead of discovering many more scrolls, archaeologists simply tore apart existing parchments to increase the finder's fee. Similar incentives were offered in China during the 19th century: farmers found several dinosaur bones on their land and then broke them apart to cash them in as rewards. Modern company boards offer bonuses when targets are met and managers spend their energy trying to lower targets instead of growing their business.

These instances illustrate Charlie Munger's famous observation about incentives causing super-response tendencies. People respond to incentives by doing what is in their best interests. What's remarkable, however, is how quickly and significantly people's behaviour changes when new incentives enter or existing ones are altered; moreover, it seems as though people respond directly to incentives themselves rather than any grander intentions behind them.

Good incentive systems combine intent and reward; for instance, in Ancient Rome engineers were invited to stand beneath their bridge construction during opening ceremonies. Poor incentive systems on the other hand often obscure or even pervert the intended aim; censoring a book may only make its contents more notorious, rewarding bank employees for each loan sold can damage credit portfolios further and making CEO salaries public did nothing but increase them; nobody wanted to be perceived as "loser CEO."

Are You Wanting to Change Behavior of Individuals or Organisations? Preaching about values and visions or appealing to reason could work, but incentives often work better - they don't even need to be financial!
Everything learned can be put to good use - from good grades and Nobel Prizes, to special treatment in the afterlife.

Long before I came to understand why educated medieval nobles gave up their luxurious lives to take part in the Crusades, I struggled to comprehend what could cause well-educated nobles from this period to leave their comfortable lifestyles behind and mount horses, knowing full well the trip took at least six months and passed directly through enemy territory - yet they took the risk. After some thought and reflection I realized: incentive systems played an essential part. If they survived they could keep all their spoils of war while becoming rich men while those who died automatically became martyrs with all its benefits for them or else went straight into heaven as martyrs - making this win-win solution possible for all participants involved - making this venture profitable from day one for both parties involved if both could come home alive; either way it was win/win situation

Imagine for a second if warriors and soldiers instead charged enemies by the hour for services rendered - we would effectively be encouraging them to take as long as possible, right? So why do we pay hourly rates when hiring lawyers, architects, consultants, accountants or driving instructors? My advice: instead negotiate fixed price agreements before engaging their services.

Be wary of investment advisers endorsing specific financial products; their focus may not be your financial wellbeing but earning commission. Entrepreneurs' and investment bankers' business plans often prove worthless because vendors only have their own interests at heart; as the old saying goes 'Never ask a barber if you need a haircut.'

Keep an eye out for incentive super-response tendencies; when someone or an organisation's behavior baffles you, ask what incentives might lie behind it and you will likely be able to explain 90% of cases with ease; any remaining 10% could be passion, idiocy, psychosis or malice.

See also Motivation Crowding (ch. 56); Reciprocity (ch. 6); Overconfidence Effect (ch. 15) for additional material on motivation crowding.

Doctors, Consultants and Psychotherapists May Be Unreliable Sources for Relief

Regression to Mean

His back pain fluctuated between being better and worse. Some days were better than others; there would be days he felt like moving mountains, others when even minimal movement was impossible. When this became problematic - which fortunately occurred only rarely - his wife would drive him to see a chiropractor; once there, the next day would find him more mobile and would recommend him highly to all his contacts.

Another, younger man with a golf handicap of 12, raved enthusiastically about his instructor, whom he booked an hour with whenever his game faltered and soon afterwards his performance improved significantly.

An investment adviser from a major bank created a bizarre 'rain dance', performing it every time his stocks performed badly in the restroom. Although it seemed absurd at the time, he felt compelled to do it; and things always improved afterwards.

What links the three men together is an error known as regression-to-mean delusion.

Say your region has experienced an unusually cold period; chances are, temperatures will gradually return towards their monthly average in coming days. The same is likely to hold true with extreme heat, drought or rain: weather fluctuates around a mean. Weather is just one indicator; so too are chronic pain, golf handicaps, stock market performance, luck in love, subjective happiness levels and test scores - they all fluctuate around some type of mean. And similarly for chronic back pain relief without chiropractic visits; handicaps returning to 12 without lessons being added in; investment advisor performance returning towards an average market performance - regardless of any restroom dances!

Extreme performances are interspersed with less extreme ones. Even the most successful stock picks from three years ago won't likely remain so in three more. You can understand why some athletes would rather avoid making headlines.
Newspapers often report top results, yet subconsciously know that next time around they may not achieve similar top results - something which has nothing to do with media attention; but is due to natural variations in performance.

Or consider the case of a division manager seeking to boost employee morale by sending the least motivated 3% of his workforce on a course, only for motivation levels not to return as before (those that had participated no longer make up this percentage - there will likely be others instead of themselves at the bottom). Was the course worth it? Hard to say since motivation levels would likely return back to their norm even without training; similar to patients hospitalised for depression who often leave feeling somewhat better but it may very well have made no contribution at all!

Example 2: In Boston, low-performing schools were placed into an intensive support programme. Within one year, their performance had improved - something authorities attributed directly to this effort rather than natural regression towards mean.

Regressing to mean can have destructive consequences, leading teachers (or managers) to believe that discipline is better than praise, for instance by rewarding high performers while punishing low achievers following tests. As a result, teachers may conclude that reproach helps and praise hinders - creating a repeating cycle where punishment helps and praise hinders performance - so their belief becomes "reproach helps and praise hinders," giving rise to another fallacy that cannot be avoided.

Conclusion: When hearing stories such as, 'I got sick, visited my doctor, and gradually improved' or 'Our company experienced difficulties over the year; therefore we hired a consultant and now results have returned to normal', it could be indicative of regression-to-mean error.

See also Problem with Averages (ch. 55); Contrast Effect (ch. 10); It Will Get Worse Before It Gets Better Fallacy (ch. 12); Coincidence (ch. 24); Gambler's Fallacy (ch. 29)

OUTCOME BIAS

Imagine one million monkeys investing on the stock market; buying and selling stocks seemingly randomly - what happens? After one week, approximately half will have made a profit while half have experienced losses. Only those monkeys that made a profit may stay; any who made losses should be sent home. After one week, half will still be riding high while half have experienced losses and must be sent away; this cycle continues throughout. After 10 weeks, approximately 1000 monkeys will remain who have consistently invested their funds wisely. After 20 weeks, only one will remain and this monkey - we will refer to as the Success Monkey - consistently chose stocks with which it could profit and is now a billionaire! Let's call him.

How will the media react? They will pounce upon this animal in search of its "success principles", and will no doubt find some: perhaps the monkey eats more bananas than his fellow primates; maybe he sits in another corner of his cage; maybe he swings through branches headlong, taking long, thoughtful pauses when grooming himself; surely some secret ingredient must exist that allows this brilliant performer to go twenty weeks unfaltering? Impossible!

The monkey story illustrates outcome bias: we tend to judge decisions by their results rather than processes, often known as historian error. A classic example of this fallacy would be Japan's attack on Pearl Harbor; should its military base have been evacuated before being attacked? Today: Yes. Evidence was overwhelming of an imminent attack; however, only in retrospect are the signals apparent. At the time, 1941 provided many contradictory signals pointing toward an attack; some indicated it while others did not. To assess the quality of this decision at its onset (i.e. before its occurrence), only information available at that moment must be considered; anything we learn post-attack must also be factored in.

Another experiment requires you to assess three heart surgeons. In order to do this, each is asked to conduct five difficult operations on themselves in succession.
Over time, the probability of death from these procedures has stabilised at 20%. Surgeon A doesn't lose anyone during surgery while surgeon B loses one patient while with surgeon C two do. How should these three surgeons be judged against one another? If you are like most people, rating A as the best, B as second best and C as worst is simply falling prey to outcome bias - possibly due to too few samples being examined - rendering results meaningless. An accurate evaluation of a surgeon requires first an understanding of his or her field, followed by careful observation during preparation and execution of operations - in other words, you need to assess both process and result when making such evaluations.

Alternately, if there are enough patients requiring this particular surgery - 100 or 1000 operations - then you could use a larger sample size. At present it suffices to understand that for an average surgeon there is a 33% chance that no one will die, 41% chance one person dies and 20% chance two people die; that is a straightforward probability calculation and shows no huge variance between zero dead and two dead; to judge these three surgeons solely on these outcomes would be both negligent and unethical.

Conclusion: it is wise not to judge decisions solely based on the outcome, particularly when randomness or external influences play a part. A poor result does not automatically signify bad decision, vice versa. Therefore, instead of lamenting poor choices made or applauding yourself for ones which only resulted in success accidentally or through coincidence alone, remember why you chose what you did; were your reasons rational and understandable? If this method worked before but didn't produce results this time around - stick with it and see where else it may lead!

See also Sunk Cost Fallacy (Ch. 5); Swimmer's Body Illusion (Ch. 2), Hindsight Bias (Ch. 14) and Illusion of Skill (Ch. 94) as related concepts.

WHY LESS IS MORE

Since my sister and her husband purchased an unfinished house recently, all we can talk about is bathroom tiles: ceramic, granite, marble, metal, stone, wood glass laminate. My sister often exclaims "There are just too many to choose from", throwing her hands up in exasperation before turning back to the catalogue as her go-to source of knowledge.

My research shows that my local grocery store stocks 48 varieties of yogurt, 134 types of red wine and 64 cleaning products for a grand total of 30,000 items; Amazon currently boasts two million titles available to them online bookseller. People today face many options from mental disorders to careers to holiday destinations and lifestyle choices - there has never been so much choice available to them!

At my childhood home in Switzerland, there were only three types of yogurt, three television channels, two churches, two types of cheese (mild or strong), trout as the only fish available and one telephone provided by Swiss Post - with its single dial serving only to make calls - making life simpler for us than today's storefronts crammed full of brands, models and contract options!

But selection is the yardstick of progress; it sets us apart from planned economies and the Stone Age. While abundance can make you happy, when exceeded it can ruin the quality of life - this phenomenon is known as paradox of choice.

Psychotherapist Barry Schwartz details in his book of the same title why this is true. A large selection can lead to inner paralysis; to demonstrate this effect, one supermarket set up a stand where customers could sample 24 types of jelly, which they could try before purchasing at a discounted rate. On day two of their experiment using six flavors instead, sales skyrocketed tenfold. Why? Perhaps having so much variety makes the decision-making process overwhelming?
Customers could not make up their minds, so they walked out without purchasing anything. This experiment was repeated several times with various products; each time, however, produced similar results.

Second, broad selection can lead to poor decisions. When asked by young people what qualities make an ideal life partner, many cite intelligence, good manners, warmth, the ability to listen, humour and physical attractiveness as priorities. But are these criteria actually taken into consideration when choosing someone? In the past, young men from villages of average size could choose among perhaps twenty girls in their school age group that he could consider for marriage. He knew their families, leading him to make a decision based on a number of shared characteristics. Now in the age of online dating, there are millions of potential partners available to us all. Studies have proven that male brains become overwhelmed with the overwhelming selection of potential partners that their selection process narrows to only one criteria: physical attractiveness. You are probably well acquainted with this selection process from your personal experiences or through media reporting.

Large selection can lead to discontent. How can you be certain you're making the appropriate choice when 200 options bombard and perplex you? You simply cannot. With more choices at your fingertips comes more uncertainty and ultimately dissatisfaction afterward.

So what should you do? Think carefully about your desired criteria before searching available offers, then stick firmly to them. Also keep in mind that perfect decisions cannot exist given the vastness of choices out there; aim for good enough rather than perfectionism instead! Rather, appreciate 'good enough' choices -- which could include life partners (but only you and me can pick exactly those we want!).

See Decision Fatigue (ch. 53); Alternative Blindness (ch. 71) and Default Effect (ch. 81) for further reading.

YOU LIKE ME A LOT; WOULDN'T YOU JUST LIKE TO TELL ME THAT??!

Kevin recently made an impulse purchase of two boxes of fine Margaux wine. Though he does not typically drink Bordeaux wines, he was so charmed by their sales assistant; not fake or pushy but truly approachable that he decided to purchase two cases as gifts for someone special.

Joe Girard is widely considered the world's top car salesman. His mantra for success: 'There is nothing more effective in selling anything than convincing customers they matter and that you truly appreciate them as people' Rather than simply talk the talk, Girard uses cards with one sentence read aloud from them every month to show his affection: I like you'

The phenomenon of liking bias is astoundingly straightforward to grasp yet we frequently fall prey to it. Simply put, it means this: the more we like someone, the more likely we are to buy or assist that individual. Yet one may ask what exactly constitutes "likeable". According to research, we perceive people as pleasing if they A) possess attractive features, B) possess similar backgrounds or interests as ourselves and C) share our interests. Advertising often features attractive people. Ugly people come across as unfriendly and don't even make the cut (see A). Advertising also employs "people like us", namely those similar in appearance, accent or background - the more similar the better! Mirroring is an effective sales technique used to achieve exactly this effect. Here, the salesperson attempts to mirror the gestures, language and facial expressions of his prospective client to achieve maximum effect. If a buyer speaks slowly and quietly while often scratching his head, it would make sense for the seller to do the same, thus increasing his chances of closing a business deal. Advertisers frequently employ compliments as part of their sales pitch: how often have you heard ads say something like: 'you deserve this!'? Again, factor C comes into play here - people find us more attractive if they like us; compliments work magic even if they ring false.

Multilevel marketing (selling through personal networks) relies solely on its ability to appeal to liking. Even though there are superior plastic containers on the market, multilevel marketing still works by taking advantage of liking.
Tupperware boasts an annual turnover of two billion dollars, due to its affordable retail prices and friendly parties hosted by friends who meet both congeniality standards perfectly.

Aid agencies use the liking bias to their advantage. Campaigns feature smiling children or women almost exclusively; never will you see a stone-faced, wounded guerrilla fighter staring back from billboards even though he also needs your support. Conservation organisations employ similar techniques; look no further than any World Wildlife Fund brochure featuring spiders, worms, algae or bacteria as the stars - even though these endangered creatures might be just as crucial to ecosystem as pandas, gorillas, koalas or seals! But we feel nothing for these creatures - instead we connect more strongly with creatures that act similarly and act similar to us than something extinct like bone skipper fly is extinct... that's too bad!

Politicians are masters at creating an atmosphere of liking among their audiences. Based on demographic and interests analysis, they tailor messages according to residential area, social background or economic issues - and flatter us: each potential voter is made to feel indispensable, hearing words like: 'Your vote counts!' and even then only by the tiniest fraction - sometimes borderline irrelevant!

One of my friends who deals in oil pumps related to pipelines told me about how he successfully closed an eight-figure deal for a pipeline in Russia without using any bribery to close it. "Bribery?" I inquired, to which my friend replied no: they started chatting about sailing and suddenly discovered we both loved 470 dinghy sailing! From thereon in, their deal was complete with amicability being far superior than bribery."

So if you are a salesperson, make your buyers think you like them by flattery or other means. On the consumer side of things, always judge products objectively regardless of who sold it to them - banishing salespeople from your mind by pretending not to like them!
See Reciprocity (ch. 6); Personification (ch. 87) for further reading on these subjects.

DO NOT Cling To Things / DO Not Adhere Tightly to Things

Endowment Effect I was stunned when I saw the BMW that stood proud in the parking lot of a used-car dealership, sparkling like new with just a few miles on its odometer and looking as good as new. To me it seemed worth around $40,000. Unfortunately, however, its salesman wanted $50k and wouldn't budge an inch on price. I decided to go for it when he called back the following week and said he would accept $40,000 instead, taking it out on its first spin that day and stopping at a gas station where the owner came out admiring my car - only for him then to offer me $53,000 cash right then and there! Needless to say, I politely declined. On my drive home, it became apparent to me how ridiculous my decision had been: an item worth $40,000 had come into my possession and instantly become worth more than $53,000! If my thinking had been pure rationality-driven, however, the car would have been sold immediately - but unfortunately for me, due to something known as the endowment effect (where objects become more valuable once owned), and therefore we tend to charge more when selling an item than we would if purchasing directly ourselves.

Psychotherapist Dan Ariely conducted an experiment to test this theory: in one of his classes, he raffled tickets to a major basketball game and polled students to gauge their valuation of them; empty-handed students estimated around $170; however winning students would never sell their ticket below an average selling price of $2,400 - ownership being associated with higher selling prices than expected.

Real estate has long demonstrated the endowment effect. Sellers become emotionally attached to their houses, which often causes them to overestimate its worth and expect buyers to pay more than what the market price allows - something which simply cannot happen as this excess represents sentimental value alone.

Richard Thaler conducted an eye-opening classroom experiment at Cornell University to measure the endowment effect. He distributed coffee mugs randomly to half of his students, telling them they could either take or sell it at their desired price point; those without one were then asked how much they would be willing to pay for one; in short, Thaler measured what is known as endowment effect.
Setup a market for coffee mugs. One would assume that roughly 50% of students would trade, either selling or buying. But the result was much lower; only 1 out of 4 owners sold below $5.25 while buyers typically would not pay more than $2.25 per mug.

One can safely say that humans are better at collecting things than discarding them, which explains both why we collect so much clutter in our homes and why collectors of stamps, watches and art rarely part with their valuable possessions.

Amazingly, the endowment effect extends not only to possession but also near-ownership. Auction houses like Christie's and Sotheby's thrive off this phenomenon: people bidding until the final minute feel that an object is practically theirs and are willing to pay much more than planned; any withdrawal from bidding is seen as a loss despite all logic. Large auctions, such as those for mining rights or mobile radio frequencies often display "the winner's curse", wherein an initial winner actually ends up losing out economically when caught up by bidding fervor and overbids. For more insight into this topic please refer back to chapter 35!

There's an analogous phenomenon in the job market. If you apply for a job and don't receive any feedback or are rejected at an interview stage, your disappointment can be intensified even more so by becoming emotionally invested in what could have been an otherwise routine selection process. Either you get the job or don't; nothing else should matter.

Conclusion: Don't become attached to physical objects; view them as temporary gifts from the universe that could disappear quickly without notice. Keep this in mind and enjoy what little time remains.

See also House-Money Effect (ch. 84); Sunk Costs Fallacy (ch. 5); Winner's Curse (ch. 35); Contrast Effect (ch. 10); Loss Aversion (ch. 32); Cognitive Dissonance (ch. 50); Not-Invented-Here Syndrome (ch. 74) and Fear of Regret (ch. 82)

COINCIDENCE

On 1 March 1950 at 7.15p.m. in Beatrice, Nebraska the 15 members of a church choir were scheduled for rehearsal. Due to various reasons they all ran behind schedule; particularly so as the minister's family were delayed ironing their daughter's dress. At 7.25p.m., church exploded, sending shockwaves through the village and shattering walls and roof. Miraculously no one was killed in the blast attributed by fire chief to gas leak, even if members of choir believed it to be divine intervention or just sheer coincidence.

Something last week reminded me of Andy, an old school friend whom I hadn't spoken with in awhile. To my amazement and surprise, my phone rang just then with no other caller than Andy on it! 'You must be telepathic!' was my exclamation in excitement as I picked it up to answer it... But was this coincidence or telepathy?

On 5 October 1990, The San Francisco Examiner reported that Intel would sue its rival AMD in court after discovering they planned to release a computer chip with an acronym known as AM386, clearly alluding to Intel's 386 chip. Intel was only aware of AMD's intentions through sheer chance: both companies employed someone named Mike Webb; both men checked out of the same hotel on the same day after staying together; reception received a package meant for Mike Webb but sent it instead to Intel instead, where it was forwarded on immediately for legal analysis and action taken against AMD immediately by legal department lawyers from legal departments of both companies.

How probable are tales such as these? Swiss psychiatrist C.G. Jung saw in them evidence of an invisible force which he called synchronicity; how should rational thinkers approach such stories? Preferably with paper and pencil; for instance in the church explosion case consider drawing four boxes to represent potential outcomes, the first being what actually took place: choir delayed and church exploded (in reality); these four boxes can then represent four possible events: (1) choir delayed before church explosion occurred (2) possible choir delays without explosion happening (3) possible choir cancellation events occurring between choir delays before church exploded (in reality this was exactly what took place) before its destruction (choir delayed rehearsal, church explosion). There are four possible possibilities when approaching such accounts with paper and pencil: 1) Choir delayed rehearsal then church explosion happened (i.e
Estimate the frequencies of these events and write them in their corresponding boxes, paying special attention to how often 'choir on time and church did not explode' has occurred; note how frequently millions of choirs meet for rehearsal and don't encounter similar circumstances as what took place in Beatrice, Nebraska (which could happen once every

century or more based on statistical probabilities), so there can be no divine intervention (besides, it seems rather silly for God to want to blow a church up!)

Apply this thinking to phone calls: think about all of the times 'Andy' thinks of you but doesn't call; when you think of him but he doesn't call; or when neither of you thinks of them but they still call?...There could be any number of instances when neither one thinks of each other at all - yet one eventually does pick up and calls, especially with 100 friends to choose from!

Estimating probabilities can be tricky. When someone says, "never", I usually register this as an estimate higher than zero as "never" can never be compensated by negative probabilities.

So let's not get carried away: unlikely coincidences are indeed unlikely but entirely possible events; their appearance should come as no shock; what would be surprising would be if they never materialized.

See also: False Causality (ch. 37); Confirmation Bias (chs 7-8); Regression to Mean (ch 19); Illusion of Control (ch 17) and Clustering Illusions (ch 3).

Have you ever experienced groupthink in a meeting? Certainly. Sitting there, quietly nodding along, hoping not to be the perpetual voice of disagreement is tough when everyone around is agreeing, so you decide against speaking up. Unfortunately, groupthink is at play here: when all members act this way they make reckless decisions because all align their opinions with what appears to be consensus despite individual members knowing better; in turn this results in motions being passed that would otherwise not have passed without peer pressure involved - an effect we discussed extensively in Chapter 4.

In March 1960, the U.S. Secret Service began recruiting anti-Communist exiles living in Miami from Cuba as weapons against Fidel Castro's regime. Just days after taking office President Kennedy was informed about this secret plan to invade Cuba. Three months later, at a crucial White House meeting attended by Kennedy and his advisers, all voted in favour of an invasion. On 17 April 1961, 1,400 exiled Cubans landed at Bay of Pigs on Cuba's south coast with support from U.S. Navy, Air Force and CIA forces. At first, everything went as planned in their attempt to overthrow Castro's government. On day one however, no supply ships reached Cuba; two were sunk by Cuban air forces before two more returned back home - all turned back, turning around, or fleeing back towards America altogether. On day two Castro surrounded and destroyed their brigade entirely. On the third day, all 1,200 survivors were captured and detained at military prisons. President Kennedy's invasion of the Bay of Pigs is widely regarded as one of the worst blunders in American foreign policy; its conception and implementation seem absurd even now. All assumptions in favor of invasion were false; for instance, Kennedy and his team underestimated Cuba's air force by an immense margin. As part of its emergency strategy, it was also intended that, should an outbreak arise, the brigade could escape to Escambray Mountains and wage underground warfare against Castro from there. A quick look at a map shows this potential safe haven was 100 miles from Bay of Pigs - providing plenty of cover.
But Kennedy and his advisors possessed remarkable intelligence for leading an American government. So what went wrong between January and April 1961?

Psychology professor Irving Janis has conducted extensive studies of numerous fiascos. He found a common theme: close-knit groups develop team spirit by (unwittingly) creating illusions. One such delusion is a sense of invincibility: If both our leader [Kennedy] and group are confident in our plan working, then luck should come our way. Unanimity also helps create this delusion: when everyone agrees on something, any divergent views must be invalid. No one likes being the person who disrupts team unity. Individuals generally appreciate being included, so expressing objections could mean exclusion; such banishment would likely spell death for our species, hence our strong instinct to remain part of a group.

Groupthink in business is nothing new, as evidenced by Swissair. Here, a group of highly paid consultants rallied behind its former CEO and developed a high-risk expansion strategy (which included purchasing several European airlines). As their zealousness built an overwhelming consensus within their team, even rational reservations were suppressed until its collapse in 2001.

If you ever find yourself in an environment in which everyone agrees on everything, speaking up should not only be tolerated but welcomed; question tacit assumptions even at risk of expulsion may also help break up stagnant thinking and establish meaningful dialogue. As leader, consider assigning someone as devil's advocate. While she might not be the most popular member, but could prove most beneficial.

See also: Social Proof (ch. 4); Social Loafing (ch. 33); In-Group Out-Group Bias (ch. 79) and Planning Fallacy (ch. 91).

WHY YOU'LL SOON BE PLAYING MEGATRILLIONS

NEGLECT OF PROBABILITY

Imagine two games of chance where each offers you an equal chance at winning $10 million; which would you pick? Winning the first would transform your life; you could quit your job, fire your boss and live off of your winnings; in contrast, winning $10,000 would give you time off work while taking an unforgettable vacation to the Caribbean without fear that soon afterward, your postcard arrives back at work - the odds for both being one in 100 million, respectively - so which would you pick? The probability for each is 1/10000! Which game do you pick?

Emotions often cause us to choose one game over the other despite objective evaluation of their odds (expected win times probability). Thus, the trend has been toward ever-larger jackpots like Mega Millions, Mega Billions, or Mega Trillions regardless of small odds involved.

In an experiment conducted in 1972, participants were divided into two groups; those assigned to one were informed they may experience an electric shock while those in the second were told there was only a 50% risk that this would happen. Researchers took measures of physical anxiety (heart rate, nervousness and sweating) shortly before beginning. What they discovered was staggering: there was absolutely no difference in stress levels across either group - all participants in both were equally overwhelmed with worry. Subsequently, researchers announced a series of decreases in shock probability for the second group: from 50% down to 20% and then 10% and finally 5%. Yet no difference could be noted! However, when both groups were told they were going to increase the strength of the expected current, anxiety levels rose again - to roughly the same degree. This shows how we react to events based on expected magnitude rather than their likelihood; we lack an intuitive grasp of probability.

Neglect of probability leads to mistakes in decision-making. We invest in start-ups because their potential profits draw our interest, yet neglect (or are too lazy) to investigate whether new businesses actually achieve such growth. Or following extensive media coverage of a plane crash, we cancel flights without fully considering our options.
Since crashing is unlikely to occur (and therefore does not change their returns), amateur investors often compare investments solely based on yield - for example, Google shares with an expected 20% return are seen as twice as desirable than property with 10% returns in their minds. Unfortunately, that approach overlooks risks, something our natural intuition does not tell us to consider properly.

Back to the experiment involving electric shocks: in Group B, the probability of receiving an electric shock was gradually decreased from 5% to 4% to 3% until its probability reached zero; only then did group B react differently from Group A; this seemed infinitely preferable than risking even just 1%!

Let's put this to the test by considering two approaches to treating drinking water. Assume a river has two equally large tributaries, both treated using methods A and B that lower risks from dying due to contamination by 5 percentage points to 2 percentage points respectively; and B that reduces it from 1 percentage point down to zero, eliminating it completely i.e. eliminating threat completely altogether. It would seem sensible for most people to go with B; however this would be silly given that with measure A three times less people die than with B; while method A is three times better! This fallacy is known as zero-risk bias

An iconic example is the U.S. Food Act of 1958, which banned foods containing cancer-causing agents to achieve zero cancer risks. Although initially effective, this ban led to more dangerous (but non-carcinogenic) food additives being introduced. Paracelsus demonstrated in the sixteenth century that poisoning is always a matter of dosage, making any law prohibiting poisoning essentially ineffectual as there would be no way of eliminating every banned molecule from food products. Every farm would need to function like a hyper-sterile computer chip factory and the cost of food would skyrocket; economically speaking, zero risk rarely makes sense; with exceptions being deadly viruses escaping biotech labs or severe storms destroying an agricultural crop.

Human beings lack an intuitive grasp of risk and therefore distinguish poorly between threats. We perceive an increase in risk as less reassuring when dealing with an emotional topic like radioactivity; two researchers from the University of Chicago have demonstrated this finding.
Fear of contamination by toxic chemicals is often an irrational response; yet it remains an understandable one.

See also Availability Bias (ch. 11); Base-Rate Neglect (ch. 28), Problem With Averages (ch. 55), Survivorship Bias (ch. 1), Illusion of Control (ch. 17) Exponential Growth (Ch 34) and Ambiguity Aversion (Ch 80).

WHY IS THE LAST COOKIE IN THE JAR MAKING MOUTH WATER

At my friend's house for coffee one evening, her three children began wrestling on the floor and we tried our hardest to engage them in conversation while their bodies fought over who would get one last marble from my bag of glass marbles - I remembered I had brought some and spread them out in hopes they'd play peacefully together; much to my disbelief, a heated argument broke out! What had occurred was completely unexpected: among all the many blue marbles was just one blue one that the children scrambled after; all other marbles had exactly equal sizes and brightness but the one blue marble had an advantage due to being one-of-one-a-kind; made me laugh out loud at how childish children could be!

As soon as I heard Google would launch its email service in August 2005, I knew I wanted one (which eventually I did). At the time, though, new accounts were extremely limited and granted only upon invitation - this made my desire even greater! Not that I needed another email account (I already had four at that point); not because Gmail was superior to competition; just that not everyone had access to it and made my craving for one even greater! Looking back, this makes me smile; adults can sometimes be childish!

Rara sunt cara, as the Romans said. Rare is valuable. Indeed, humans have long suffered from this misperception of scarcity. My friend with three children works part-time as a real-estate agent; whenever she has potential buyers who cannot decide between two property options she calls and says that "A doctor from London visited it yesterday". "He liked it very much. What about you, are you still interested?"' The doctor from London (sometimes it can also be professor or banker) is obviously fictional; yet his effect can be very real: prospects see an opportunity disappear before them and act quickly to close a deal, again due to potential shortage of supply; this situation cannot be explained objectively since either they want the land at the set price or they do not; regardless of any fictitious doctors from London who might pop up.

Professor Stephen Worchel divided participants into two groups for testing cookie quality: one received an entire box while the second only got some.
Subgroup B included only two cookies; when asked to rate their quality, these subjects far outshone those from Group 1. The experiment was repeated several times with similar results each time.

Adverts often tout, "Only while stocks last." Posters frequently warn us to act quickly when scarcity errors arise. Gallery owners take advantage of this error by placing red'sold' dots under most paintings, making the remaining few rare and desirable pieces even more desirable and thus creating scarcity errors that should be snatched up quickly before they become scarcer items that must be snapped up quickly. Stamp collectors, coin enthusiasts, vintage car enthusiasts alike often collect stamps, coins and cars even though these no longer serve a practical use - the attraction stemming from scarcity errors rather than anything practical! This all adds up.

Students were instructed to arrange 10 posters according to attractiveness - with the understanding that afterward they could keep one as a reward for participating. Five minutes later they were informed that one had not been available - with three being unavailable due to being pulled back out by security personnel. After that, they were asked to review all ten posters from scratch, with one poster that no longer existed suddenly becoming the most beautiful one. Psychologists refer to this phenomenon as reactance: when faced with choices we cannot have, our brain often reacts by assigning greater attractiveness to alternatives that no longer exist - an act of defiance against loss of control over an option. Romeo and Juliet effect is well known: forbidden romance between Shakespearean teenagers leads them to an irrepressible yearning that knows no boundaries. Not necessarily romantic in nature - in America student parties are filled with desperate drunken students due to underage drinking laws being prohibited.

Conclusion: In response to scarcity, most people tend to make decisions with little clear thinking. When making purchases and decisions based solely on cost-benefit analysis, any signs that an item might be quickly disappearing should not matter; nor should London doctors take an interest.
Notes on Contrast Effect (ch. 10); Fear of Regret (ch. 82) and House-Money Effect (ch. 84)
For further insight, when hearing hoofbeats do not expect a zebra!

BASE-RATE NEGLECT

Imagine Mark is a thin man from Germany wearing glasses who likes listening to Mozart. Is he most likely either: A) a truck driver in Germany, or B) a professor of literature in Frankfurt? Most will guess B, which would be incorrect as Germany has 10,000 times more truck drivers than literature professors - meaning he should more likely be an trucker! Our minds were fooled by detailed description leading us away from statistical reality; scientists refer to this error of logic as base-rate neglect which leads us away from considering fundamental distribution levels - one of our most frequent errors of reasoning! Many journalists, economists and politicians regularly fall victim to it resulting in wrong decisions being taken when making assumptions regarding which outcome may occur from our assumptions regarding fundamental distribution levels being ignored when making decisions that might lead us down this road!

Here is another scenario in which a young man is fatally stabbed: which option is more likely? A) An attacker could be an illegal Russian immigrant importing combat knives illegally, or B) An attacker is from middle class America importing these knives illegally - option B is much more likely given there are millions more middle-class Americans than there are Russian knife importers.

Base-rate neglect plays a pivotal role in medicine. Migraines, for instance, could indicate anything from viral infection or brain tumor to heart problems; doctors usually assess for viral infections first before testing for tumors to ensure patient wellbeing. Medical school residents spend considerable time purging base-rate neglect; one motto often repeated to future doctors in the US is 'When you hear hoofbeats behind you don't expect to see a zebra!' which means: investigate more likely ailments first before diagnosing exotic ones even if that specialty requires you.

Doctors are the only professionals with access to such extensive training; unfortunately, few people in business receive such an introduction. I often become excited when reading high-flying entrepreneur business plans that could become the next Google! Yet upon closer examination I realize the probability that their firm will survive its first five years is only 20%; hence their likelihood of survival must also reflect this reality.
Warren Buffett once explained why he doesn't invest in biotech companies: 'How many of these firms make turnover of several hundred million dollars? It simply does not happen?...?The most likely scenario for these firms will likely remain somewhere in the middle.' This is clear base-rate thinking. Most people's base-rate neglect can be attributed to survivorship bias (chapter 1): they tend to only see successful individuals and companies

since unsuccessful cases tend to go unreported (or underreported), thus leading them to overlook those more 'invisible' cases that exist within.

Imagine this: when tasting wine at a restaurant, the label on each bottle has been removed, leaving only an indicator as to its origins: France is typically three quarters of wines on offer so, without knowing better, most likely you would choose France over Chilean or Californian options.

Sometimes I have the unfortunate pleasure of speaking in front of students from prestigious business schools. When asked about their career goals, many answer that in the medium term they see themselves on boards of global companies - similar answers were given by my fellow students when we attended. When given this information, students usually respond that with a degree from this school the chances of landing a Fortune 500 company board spot is less than 0.1% - that most likely they'll end up somewhere within middle management instead - which always garners shocked looks but I think that I made some small contribution towards mitigating their future midlife crises!
See also:hesitez 1 26 Gambler's Fallacy (ch. 29); Conjunction Fallacy (ch. 41); Problem with Averages (ch. 55) Information Bias (ch 59); Ambiguity Aversion (ch 8) (Baloney Theory 29 - A Proven Fact).

Gambler's Fallacy Something remarkable occurred in Monte Carlo during 1913: large crowds gathered around a roulette table were amazed to witness its ball landing on black twenty times consecutively! Players took full advantage of this phenomenon, quickly placing money on red, but yet another time the ball came to rest on black despite more people betting red than before - until finally on its twenty-seventh spin, when the ball finally settled on red - leaving millions staked and players bankrupt within minutes.

Imagine this: the average IQ of pupils in a big city is 100. To investigate this further, you take a random sample of 50 students with one child tested having an IQ of 150 and observe their progress over several months. Most people guess 100; perhaps thinking the super-smart student will be offset by either someone having an average IQ of 50 or two below-average students having 75 IQs respectively - however this scenario is highly unlikely; rather we must expect that each of our remaining 49 will represent their population by each having an average IQ of 100 giving us an average score of 101 for your 50 students.

Monte Carlo and IQ experiments demonstrate how people tend to believe that there is an invisible 'balancing force of the universe'; this is known as gambler's fallacy. With independent events however, there is no such force: balls cannot remember how often they land on black. Yet one of my friends enters his weekly Mega Millions numbers into an Excel spreadsheet before playing those that have appeared least often -- all this work for nothing - he too falls victim of gambler's fallacy!

A joke illustrates this phenomenon: A mathematician who fears flying due to its risk of terrorist attack takes every flight with a bomb in his hand luggage in case something should happen on board; with this measure in place, his probability of having one onboard increases significantly.
"The chances of two bombs being on one plane are exceedingly remote!" He further states.

Imagine being forced to spend thousands of dollars of your own money betting on the outcome of the next coin toss, each time landing with heads each time. Given this scenario, many people would likely choose tails even though heads is equally likely. Gambler's fallacy makes us believe something must change!

Once again, someone forces you to place a bet. Do you pick heads or tails this time around? Now that you've seen some examples, you are familiar with the game; knowing it could go either way. Unfortunately, we've just come upon another pitfall of mathematicians' deformation professionnelle (professional oversight); logic tells you heads is likely the wiser option as the coin appears rigged against tails.

Recent articles examined regression to mean. As an illustration, consider this scenario: If your area is experiencing record cold, chances are the temperature will return to normal values over the coming days - just like in a casino! Complex feedback mechanisms in the atmosphere ensure extremes balance themselves out over time while extremes sometimes intensify - for instance when rich people get richer, and stocks that explode create additional demand due to standing out - creating something of a reverse compensation effect.

Be mindful of both independent and interdependent events in your environment. Purely independent events only exist in casinos, lotteries and theoretical settings - these may exist at casinos, lotteries or theoretical levels; real life often presents us with interrelated events which influence one another - think financial markets or health. Past events have an influence over future ones. As comforting an idea may sound, there simply is no balancing force out there to protect independent events against negative influences; no such 'what goes around, comes around' concept exists either!
See also: Averages (ch. 55); Base-Rate Neglect (ch. 28); Deformation Professionnelle (ch. 92); Regression to the Mean (ch. 19); Simple Logic (ch. 63) for additional discussion of these subjects. 29

WHY THE WHEEL OF FORTUNE MAKES US SPIRAL?

Where was Abraham Lincoln born? Without immediate access to an answer and with your smartphone battery having just run out, how would you answer such a question? Perhaps knowing he served as President during the American Civil War 1860s and that he became the first U.S. president ever assassinated is enough for you? Viewing the Lincoln Memorial in Washington doesn't conjure images of an energetic young person but more along the lines of an aged veteran at 60 years old. Since he was assassinated sometime between 1860-1864 (he died 1809), 1805 is our estimated year for birth (it should actually be 1809). How did we figure this out? By using an anchor point like 1865 as our starting point and working backward from there to make an educated estimate.

When we need to guess something - for instance the length of the Mississippi River, population density in Russia or nuclear power plant numbers in France - we use anchors. Starting from something familiar we explore unfamiliar territory from there. What other way could there be of doing it if not picking random numbers off our heads? That would be completely irrational!

Unfortunately, anchors can also be misused. For example, in one lecture class a professor had his students write down the last two digits of their social security numbers before making decisions about whether to bid on a bottle of wine at auction based on those figures - leading them to bid nearly twice more if their number was higher compared with lower ones! Thus demonstrating how social security numbers act as an anchor; even if in an indirect or deceptive fashion.

Psychologe Amos Tversky conducted an experiment using a wheel of fortune. Participants would spin it, and afterwards were asked how many member states the United Nations has; their guesses confirmed the anchor effect: individuals who had spun high numbers on the wheel had given higher estimates than people who hadn't spun as high a number on it.

Russo and Shoemaker conducted research aimed at uncovering when Attila the Hun was defeated in Europe - similar to asking students what year social security began its roll out. Participants were then given anchor points based on the last few digits of their telephone number, with those with higher numbers choosing later years and vice versa (Attila was killed off in 453)

Anchors abound, and we all cling to them. For instance, many products contain an advertised "recommended retail price", acting as an anchor point. Sales professionals know they must establish prices early - long before an offer has been presented - to secure sales success. Furthermore, research has demonstrated that knowing students' past grades influences how teachers mark new work - the latest grades act as a starting point.

My early years were spent at a consulting firm. My boss was adept at using anchors. In his initial conversation with any client, he would set an opening price which, by law, far outshone our internal costs: "Just so you don't get surprised when receiving your quote, Mr. So-and-So: recently completed a similar project for one of your competitors was in the range of five million dollars". That anchor then was dropped - price negotiations began at exactly this amount.

See also Framing (ch. 42).

At first, the shy animal seems skeptical; eventually however, its resistance subsides and they start eating regularly from each other. Eventually though, their suspicion gives way and eventually their trust grows stronger than before. After several months, the goose comes to believe that its farmer has its best interests at heart, as every additional day's feeding confirms this assumption. She was left dumbfounded when on Christmas Day he took it out of its enclosure - only to slaughter her instead! David Hume used an allegory involving Christmas geese as a warning against inductive thinking - the tendency to infer universal truths from individual observations. Although his tale may seem relevant only during Christmastime, its lessons extend far beyond this symbolic holiday holiday bird. But inductive reasoning affects not just geese.

An investor buys stock X and initially becomes suspicious as its share price skyrockets, suspecting a bubble may exist. But as time passes and it continues its upward trajectory, his suspicion gives way to excitement: this stock may never come down! In just half a year's time he commits all of his savings into it with little regard for the cluster risk associated with investing his life savings in it - only later to pay dearly for such foolish decisions made out of greed and ignorance.

Inductive thinking doesn't need to lead you down a path toward disaster; in fact, you could turn inductive thinking into a source of profit by sending out emails with forecasts for both rising prices next month and declining ones - one predicting they may drop. Send the first email to 50,000 people and then a separate group of 50,000 people after one month, when indices had declined significantly. Now send another email but this time only to those 50,000 people who received accurate predictions in their first email. After 10 months, around 100 of your clients will remain. From their perspective, you have proven your prophetic powers. Some will trust you with their money - take it and start living life again in Brazil.
However, we're not just fooled by naive strangers; even ourselves can be fooled; those who rarely fall ill believe themselves immortal. CEOs who post consecutive quarters of increased profits tend to think themselves unbeatable - as do their employees and shareholders. I once had a friend who enjoyed base jumping. He would launch himself off cliffs, antennae, buildings etc, only pulling his ripcord at the last moment before landing safely on earth. One day, I inquired as to the level of risk his chosen sport posed and his response was quite casual: 'I have over 1,000 jumps under my belt and nothing ever happens to me.' Two months later he had died when jumping from an especially hazardous cliff in South Africa - this tragic event disproved all theory proved repeatedly over.

Inductive thinking can have disastrous repercussions, yet we depend on it every day for survival. When we board an aircraft, aerodynamic laws remain valid; we trust that random attacks won't happen on the street; our hearts should still beat tomorrow - these are essential assurances without which life would not go on - however it must always be remembered that only certainties such as death and taxes are permanent; Benjamin Franklin said it best: 'Nothing is certain but death and taxes.'

Induction can lull us into believing things like: 'Mankind has always survived, so we will be able to face any future challenges too.' While this seems logical in theory, what many fail to acknowledge is that such statements can only come from species who have survived up until this point; making assumptions that our survival today indicates future survival would be an epic mistake and possibly the gravest reasoning error ever.

False Causality (ch.37); Survivorship Bias (ch. 1) are also covered here.

WHY DOES EVIL HIT HARDER THAN GOOD?

Loss Aversion How are you currently feeling on a scale from 1-10? Now imagine what would bring you up to 10, such as that trip to the Caribbean you've always longed for or an increase in career advancement? Keeping this exercise going: what might bring down your score by the same number? Paralysis, Alzheimer's, cancer, depression, war hunger torture financial ruin damage reputation loss friend getting kidnapped blindness death are just a few options available that would bring about great displeasure; simply thinking through all these possibilities makes us aware of just how many obstacles there exist in terms of keeping up the happiness spectrum compared with all that positive influences; all this lists highlights just how many obstacles there exist and their far more severe effects than benefits; no wonder we don't seek happiness than ever thought we did before.

At one point in our evolutionary past, this was even truer - one small mistake could lead to death instantly. Any number of things could cause your swift departure from life: careless hunting practices, tendon inflammation or exclusion from group. People who were careless or reckless often died before passing along their genes to future generations; only cautious ones survived and are our descendants today.

So it is understandable why we fear loss more than gain; losing $100 costs us far greater happiness than any joy it might bring us if I gave it to us instead. Indeed, studies have proven that an emotional response weighs twice that of any similar gain - social scientists refer to this phenomenon as loss aversion.

For this reason, when trying to convince someone of something, don't focus on its benefits; instead stress how it helps them avoid disadvantages. A campaign promoting breast self-examination (BSE) utilized two different leaflets distributed among women in order to spread information on BSE. Pamphlet A stated, 'Research indicates that women participating in BSE have an increased chance of discovering tumors at an early, more treatable stage'. Pamphlet B stated, 'Research has revealed that women who refrain from performing BSE have an increased chance of finding cancerous tumours early and more treatable stages,' The study indicated that pamphlet B's narrative (written from a "loss frame") created significantly greater awareness and behavior change than pamphlet A's (written in an "earn frame").
Fear of loss motivates people more than the prospect of gaining something of equal value, so if your business offers home insulation products, an effective way to encourage customers to purchase is by showing them how much money they could lose without insulation instead of how much they might save with it - even though both amounts would remain the same.

On the stock market, investors often ignore losses on paper as an unrealised loss is less painful than an actual one; so they remain investors even though chances for recovery or further decline may be slim. I once met a multimillionaire who was very upset that he'd lost $100 in an instant; yet his portfolio fluctuated by at least this amount every second! I tried explaining to him this emotion is unwarranted since his portfolio fluctuates every second by at least this amount!

Managers in large companies typically push employees to be bolder and more entrepreneurial, yet in reality many employees tend to be risk-averse. From their perspective, this makes sense: why risk something which could bring either an increased bonus or worse--a pink slip? In most cases and situations, career protection trumps any potential reward - so if you've been perplexed about why risk-taking among your employees seems lacking, now you know why (although when employees do take significant risks this often comes under the guise of group decisions - learn more in chapter 33 about social loafing).

Evil is more powerful and prevalent than good; we tend to react more strongly when negative things come our way than when positive ones do; scary faces tend to stand out more on the street than smiling ones; we remember bad behavior longer - except when it pertains to ourselves!
See also House-Money Effect (ch. 84); Endowment Effect (ch. 23), Social Loafing, (ch. 33) Default Effect, Sunk Cost Fallacy and Framing as well as Affect Heuristic in Chapter 42 for further insight. (CH 66) .

WHY TEAM MEMBERS ARE LAZY

Social Loafing

In 1913, French engineer Maximilian Ringelmann conducted research into horse performance. To his amazement, two horses pulling a coach did not equal twice that of one horse alone. Perplexed at this result, Ringelmann turned his research to humans; having several individuals pull ropes together at once while measuring force applied by each one individually he found that when two people pulled together they invested an average of 93% of their individual strength into pulling together; with three pulling together it dropped to 86% investment; when three pulled together just 49%!

Science refers to this phenomenon as the social loafing effect. This occurs when individual performance isn't readily noticeable - when individual contributions become blended into the collective effort rather than visible to observers directly. Social loafing often happens in rowers' races but not relay races where individual contributions become apparent. Social loafing can be rational behavior: why invest all your energy when half will do? Taking shortcuts without anyone realizing is also common practice - like Ringelmann's horses! Overall, social loafing can be seen as a form of cheating which all of us are guilty of engaging in unconsciously, just as Ringelmann did when working against them against opponents!

As people work together, individual performances tend to decrease - something which should come as no surprise - but what should stand out is our continued input despite decreasing individual performances. What keeps us from simply giving up completely and leaving all the hard work for others to do? Consequences - zero performance would be noticed and could result in serious consequences such as exclusion from a group or vilification; Evolution has given us finely tuned senses that allow us to discern how much idleness can pass undetected from ourselves or detect it in others.

Social loafing extends far beyond physical performance; we also mentally slack off. For instance, meetings where too many participants are present tend to see weaker individual participation than when only 20 or 100 are in attendance; once this threshold has been crossed however, performance levels plateau. Whether a group consists of 20 or 100 members doesn't matter as we have reached maximum inertia and reach maximum performance potential.

One nagging question remains: who originated the notion that teams outshone individuals? Perhaps Japanese. Thirty years ago.
Business economists examined Japan's industrial miracle and observed its factories being organized into teams. Business economists then attempted to copy this model with mixed success - some teams performed exceptionally well, but not others (possibly because social

loafing rarely occurred there), while in Europe teams that consisted of diverse yet specialized people performed best overall; within such groups individual performances could easily be identified and traced back.

Social loafing can have profound ramifications. Group members tend to limit both participation and accountability for group misdeeds or poor decisions. No one wants to shoulder blame alone. One egregious example is the prosecution of Nazis at the Nuremberg trials; less contentiously, consider any board or management team. We often hide behind team decisions to avoid taking responsibility; this practice is known as diffusion of responsibility. Team dynamics also cause them to take greater risks than they would take individually; members tend to believe they won't be held personally responsible if something goes wrong, which leads to risky shift. This phenomenon is particularly risky among company and pension-fund strategists with billions at stake and defence departments where groups decide when nuclear weapons should be deployed.

Conclusion: People behave differently when in groups than alone (otherwise there wouldn't be groups). The negative aspects of groups can be offset by making individual performances visible as much as possible - long live meritocracy! Long live the performance society!

Motivation Crowding (ch. 56); Social Proof (ch. 4); Groupthink (ch. 25); Loss Aversion (ch. 32)

SURROUNDED BY PAPER?

Exponential Growth

Its Imagine you are folding a sheet of paper repeatedly into two, only this time folding it again on itself - 50 times total? What do you estimate its thickness will be after folding 50 times? Make a note of your guess before continuing reading.

Second Task. Select one of two options from below. A) Over the next 30 days, I will give you $1,000 daily. B) I will give a cent daily starting with Day 1, followed by two cents on Day 2 then four cents and so forth until Day 31 arrives and your reward total reaches eight cents each day thereafter. But decide quickly between A or B?

Are You Prepared? Assuming a sheet of copy paper measures approximately 0.004 inches thick, its thickness after 50 folds becomes over 60 million miles; which equals the distance between Earth and Sun as measured with a calculator. When answering question 2, choosing option B may seem less appealing but will yield more rewards in just 30 days than A does; taking option A would give you $30,000 but B more than $5 Million!

Linear growth is intuitively grasped. But we have no sense of exponential (or percentage) growth - likely because our ancestors didn't need it before! Their experiences tended to be linear: spending double time collecting berries yielded double the earnings and killing two mammoths instead of one extended the hunt by half as long. But today, exponential growth is no longer rare! In the Stone Age people rarely encountered exponential growth. Now things are different.

"Each year, traffic accidents increase by 7%," warns a politician. To understand what this means intuitively, let's use an easy formula: 70 divided by 7 = 10 years - which indicates that traffic accidents double every decade (notes section for further explanation on why that number 70?). This would indicate an alarming scenario! If this figure seems unfamiliar to you, take note of logarithm; its definition can be found there).

Another example: Inflation stands at 5%, leading many people to think it doesn't pose too much of a threat - until one calculates the doubling time: 70 divided by 5 = 14 years, meaning in 14 years' time one dollar will only be worth half as much - an absolute disaster for anyone with savings accounts!

Imagine you're a journalist reporting that registered dog registrations in your city are rising by 10% annually; how will you tell readers this news? No one cares, so instead announce:

'Deluge of dogs: double as many mutts in 7 years!' No one will care as much - people won't care that the registrations have increased by 10% either.

Nothing that grows exponentially will continue forever; many politicians, economists and journalists forget this truth. Such growth eventually reaches its limit; for instance, Escherichia coli divides every twenty minutes and could cover the planet within days but cannot continue due to consumes more oxygen and sugar than available. Therefore its growth eventually hits an impasse point and cuts off.

Ancient Persians understood the difficulty associated with percentage growth. Here's an interesting local tale: one wise courtier presented the king with a chessboard as a gift and asked how they could thank him; his reply? Cover it with rice covering one grain on every square before increasing with two additional grains twice every square thereafter! When surprised, King Darius replied it was indeed an honor for them that such modest requests came from such worthy courtiers!

But how much rice does he need? At first he estimated about one sack. When his servants began the task - placing one grain on each square in turn until there were four grains per square and so forth - did he realize he required more grains than was available on earth.

When it comes to growth rates, do not rely on intuition - you don't have any. Accept it instead. What truly helps is using a calculator - or in cases with low growth rates using 70 as the magic number.

See also, Simple Logic (ch. 63); Neglect of Probability (ch. 26); The Law of Small Numbers (ch. 61)

WINNER'S CURSE

Texas in the 1950s. Ten oil companies compete for an auctioned plot of land valued between $10 million and $100 million; when prices escalate during bidding, more firms exit bidding until finally one company submits the highest bid and wins the auction with champagne corks popping!

The "Winner's Curse" holds that auction winners often end up as losers, as evidenced by industry analysts who noted companies that consistently came out as winning bidders from oilfield auctions overpaid and later went bankrupt - something which should come as no surprise when estimates vary between $10 million and $100 million; estimates often lie somewhere in between; often, auction high bids exceed their true worth; in Texas however, oil managers celebrated what became a costly victory after all.

Today, this phenomenon affects us all. From eBay to Groupon to Google AdWords, prices are set by auctions - from eBay to Groupon to Google AdWords; bidding wars over cellphone frequencies drive telecom companies closer to bankruptcy; airports rent their commercial spaces out for highest bidder; or when Walmart plans a detergent rollout requesting tenders from five suppliers (in effect an auction with risk associated with winning and being cursed with the winner's curse!). Even Walmart introduces products through auctions - asking suppliers for tenders from five suppliers is just another auction - only this time risking being cursed!

Internet auctioning of everyday life has spread to tradesmen as well. When I needed my walls painted, rather than searching out just any painter nearby, I posted my ad online instead - 30 painters from across 300 miles competed for it, offering such low quotes that it became impossible for me to accept - out of kindness for them all! The best offer came from one so poor that out of sympathy I declined it so as to spare him or her the winner's curse!

Initial Public Offerings (IPOs) and mergers and acquisitions, more commonly referred to as mergers and acquisitions, can also be seen as auctions. Unfortunately, more than half of acquisitions destroyed value according to one McKinsey study!
Why do we succumb to the winner's curse? There are a couple of factors at work. First, real values for many things remain uncertain. Additionally, more interested parties increase the odds of an overly enthusiastic bid being submitted. Second is competition amongst vendors; one friend owning a micro-antenna factory recounted how Apple instigated an intense bidding war for suppliers when developing the iPhone - everyone wanting an official contract even though this might mean financial losses down the road for winning suppliers.

How much would you offer for $100? Assume you and an opponent are invited to an auction whereby whoever makes the highest offer wins and both bidders must submit their final offers at that point - how high would your offer go? From your perspective, it makes sense to offer $20, $30 or $40; your opponent does the same and even $99 seems reasonable when discussing $100 bills - yet they now propose offering $100 instead! If this remains the highest bid, he will break even (paying $100 for $100), while you only need to cough up $99. As long as this remains the highest bid, both players will come away even. Thus you continue bidding. At $110 you have a guaranteed loss of $10; your opponent would need to come up with $109 (his last bid), meaning both will continue playing until one or both gives up playing altogether - when will you stop bidding and when will your competitor stop bidding? Test it with friends!

Warren Buffett offered some sound advice regarding auctions: 'Don't go.' If auctions are necessary in your industry, set a maximum price and deduct 20% from it as an offset against winner's curse; write this number down and don't exceed it in any way.

See Endowment Effect (ch. 23) for further information.

WRITERS SHOULD NEVER ASK WRITER WHETHER HIS NOVEL IS AUTOBIOGRAPHICAL

FUNDAMENTAL ATTRIBUTION ERROR

Opening your newspaper, you learn of yet another CEO being forced out due to poor results. Meanwhile, in sports section you read that player X or coach Y contributed significantly to your team's winning season, while history books tell you Napoleon was responsible for leading and leading his army so successfully in early 1800s France. "Every story has a face" seems like an inalienable rule of every newsroom; journalists (and their readers) take this principle further by looking out for any possible "people angle". As a result of this "people angle", many journalists (and readers alike) fall prey to fundamental attribution error: an error caused by overestimating individuals influence while underestimating external, situational factors.

Researchers from Duke University conducted an experiment in 1967: participants read arguments either praising or denigrating Fidel Castro from an author assigned regardless of his actual views; yet most audience members believed what he said represented his true opinions and disregarded external factors - i.e. professors who crafted it.

The Fundamental Attribution Error is particularly effective at simplifying negative events into manageable units. We often attribute blame for wars to individuals - like Yugoslav assassin in Sarajevo has World War I on their shoulders or Hitler started World War II by himself - even though wars are unpredictable events with complex dynamics we will likely never fully comprehend - much like financial markets and climate issues!

As companies announce good or bad results, all eyes tend to focus on their CEO despite knowing the truth: economic success depends far more on factors outside their control, like industry attractiveness. It is remarkable how often firms in struggling industries replace their CEO compared to how rarely this occurs in more thriving firms.
Are industries facing difficulties less careful in their recruitment practices? Such decisions do not seem any less irrational than what occurs between football coaches and their clubs.

My hometown, Lucerne in Switzerland, provides me with plenty of luscious classical recitals that never cease to impress. However, during intermission conversations tend to focus almost solely on conductors and soloists while composition rarely makes headlines; except during world premieres when composers can discuss it openly. Why is that? Music's true miracle lies in composition: its creation of sounds, moods and rhythms from seemingly nothing; however it often goes underappreciated due to our inability to consider that scores have no faces to compare against conductors and soloists when in fact these two elements make up performances of that score (unlike conductors or soloists or conductors/soloists).

As a fiction writer, I encounter this fundamental attribution error every time after giving readings (which in itself can be controversial), when people ask: 'What part of your novel is autobiographical?' At times like these I wish that I could shout back: 'It's not about me - it's about this book, text, language and story!' but my upbringing doesn't allow such outbursts often enough.

Attribution errors should not be judged harshly. Our preoccupation with other people stems from our evolutionary past: group membership was essential for survival - reproduction, defense, hunting large animals were impossible without help from one's tribe - banishment meant certain death; those opting for solo lives often faced certain doom as well.

But even those surviving ultimately left the gene pool, making life even harder on subsequent generations. Our lives depended and revolved around others; that explains why today we remain so preoccupied with them - to the point of spending about 90% of our time thinking about other people while only devoting 10% to considering other factors and contexts.

Conclusion: Though we find the spectacle of life riveting, its inhabitants are far from being ideal characters who make decisions without needing outside help. They flit from situation to situation rather than acting on their own volition. To truly understand any current play or musical, look beyond its performers and pay close attention to how influences shape actors' characters.
See also Story Bias (Ch. 13); Swimmer's Body Illusion (Ch. 2), Salience Effect (Ch. 83), News Illusion (Ch. 99), Halo Effect (Ch. 38) and Fallacy of Single Causes (Ch. 97)

WHY YOU SHOULDN'T BELIEVE WHAT THE STORYTELLER TELLS

Head lice were an integral part of life on the Hebrides islands north of Scotland, and their absence would cause their hosts to become sick and feverish. In order to combat their sickness and feverishness, sick people would intentionally add lice back into their hair so as to get rid of their fever; once these new lice had taken root and settled into place again, patients began showing improvements.

Studies conducted in one city indicated that, the more firefighters called out to fight fires, the greater its damage was. Following these results, the mayor immediately instituted an immediate hiring freeze and reduced firefighting budget accordingly.

Both stories come from German physics professors Hans-Peter Beck-Bornholdt and Hans-Hermann Dubben's book (unfortunately there is no English version). Both stories illustrate how causality can become confused; when lice leave an invalid's head because he has fever, their presence becomes temporary as hot feet kicks in; once fever has broken they return! And larger fires require more firefighters - not vice versa!

False causality often misleads us and business-book authors and consultants often operate using this misguided thinking to sell us false narratives of causality. Take for instance the headline, 'Employee motivation leads to higher corporate profits.' Does that really hold water, or might people simply become more motivated when their company does well? Similarly, another claim states that women on boards correlates to increased profitability - yet is that really how it works or are these firms simply more likely to recruit more women onto boards than less profitable firms do? These business-book authors and consultants frequently operate using similar false (or at least fuzzy) causalities when writing or consulting on business books or providing advice.

Alan Greenspan was revered as head of the Federal Reserve during the 90s. His obscure statements gave monetary policy the appearance of being an exact science which kept America on an upward path towards prosperity, drawing praise from politicians, journalists and business leaders alike. Unfortunately for these commentators though, America's close ties with China (a low-cost producer that readily bought U.S. debt) played far greater part than assumed at first; Greenspan simply got lucky that his policies worked so well.
So well did he serve his term.

Scientists recently conducted studies that suggested extended hospital stays were detrimental to patient health. This information pleased health insurers; who want stays to be brief. But longer stays don't seem detrimental at all since patients who can leave immediately are healthier than those requiring further treatments - and hence long stays may actually have positive outcomes!

Or take this headline: 'Fact: Women who use shampoo XYZ on a regular basis have stronger hair.' Although scientific evidence can support such claims, this statement doesn't really tell us much - least of all that the shampoo makes your locks stronger! Perhaps women with strong locks tend to use this particular brand - maybe because its bottle says "especially designed for thick hair".

Recently I read that students with homes containing many books tend to achieve higher grades at school. While this study may have provided booksellers a boost, this research proved false causality - more educated parents tend to place greater value on their children's education, as do educated individuals generally having more books at home; even so, one dust-covered copy of War and Peace won't change anyone's grades; what matters are both parents' educational levels as well as genes!

False causality was at its finest in Germany between birth rate and number of stork pairs in decline from 1965-1987. Both trends seemed almost correlated; could this mean the stork really brings babies? No doubt not; rather this correlation could simply have been accidental.

Conclusion: correlation does not equate to causation. Take a closer look at events linked by correlation: sometimes what seems like its cause turns out to be its effect, and vice versa; other times there may even be no apparent causal connection - like there was with storks and babies.

See also Coincidence (Ch. 24); Association Bias (Ch. 48); Clustering Illusions (Ch. 3); Story Biases (Ch. 13) * Induction (Ch. 31) and Beginner's Luck (Ch. 49)

Silicon Valley firm Cisco was once celebrated by business journalists as an icon of the new economy, receiving rave reviews for its fantastic customer service, excellent strategy, timely acquisitions, vibrant corporate culture and charismatic CEO. By March 2000 it had become the world's most valuable company.

As Cisco's stock fell 80% the following year, journalists changed their tune. Now its competitive advantages were being perceived as detrimental shortcomings: poor customer service, an unclear strategy, unwise acquisitions, lame corporate culture and an uninspiring CEO were being blamed - yet neither its strategy or CEO had changed; demand had simply decreased thanks to the dot-com crash and this change had nothing to do with them.

The "halo effect" occurs when one aspect of a whole dazzles us and alters how we perceive its entirety. Cisco was an exceptional case where this phenomenon manifested itself: journalists were floored by its stock prices and assumed its entire business to be equally remarkable without conducting thorough investigations into it further.

The halo effect typically works this way: we take an easy-to-grasp or striking detail about a company, like its financial situation, and extrapolate conclusions from there about more difficult-to-assess aspects such as management merit or feasibility of strategy. From here we draw conclusions that may or may not be accurate such as whether its management merit or strategy feasibility merit. Sometimes success and superiority is given where none is due such as when we buy products from manufacturers simply due to their good reputation - another example being believing CEOs from one industry will flourish across other sectors while being heroes both within their personal lives too!

Edward Lee Thorndike discovered the "halo effect" nearly 100 years ago. His observation was that an individual quality (beauty, social status or age) can create either positive or negative perceptions that overwhelm all else - such as looks. Research has confirmed this finding through numerous studies confirming our bias toward good-looking people as more pleasant, honest and intelligent; attractive people also often enjoy greater success in life overall.
These results do not correlate with any myth of women'sleeping their way to success'; indeed, teachers unintentionally give attractive students higher grades than less attractive ones.

Advertising has found an ally in the form of the halo effect: just think of all of the celebrities we see smiling back from TV ads, billboards and magazines. What makes professional tennis players like Roger Federer such an expert on coffee machines remains uncertain;

nevertheless it hasn't detracted from their campaigns' success. As we become used to seeing celebrities supporting arbitrary products without questioning why their support might matter so much; this is precisely how the halo effect works: subconsciously. All that needs to register in our minds is attractive faces with dream lifestyles associated with that product - then boom - boom - success!

On the negative side, the halo effect can lead to great injustice and stereotyping when nationality, gender or race becomes the focal point. No need to be racist or sexist: just let the halo effect cloud our view; journalists, educators and consumers all too easily fall prey.

Have you ever experienced falling in love? If so, then you understand the exhilaration of finding that "one perfect person." They seem attractive, intelligent, likable and warm - while other might point out obvious faults; all you see are endearing quirks!

To reduce this halo effect and gain clarity into true characteristics, look beyond face value to eliminate most striking features that draw your eye. Orchestras often do this by screening candidates in front of a screen so sex, race, age and appearance do not play into their decisions; business journalists should do likewise and consider looking beyond quarterly figures (the stock market already provides that). Dig deeper - investing time and energy in research often yields unexpected but often educational findings.

See Also: Fundamental Attribution Error (ch. 36); Salience Effect (ch. 83); Swimmer's Body Illusion (ch. 2) Contrast Effect (ch. 10); Expectations (ch. 62)

Congratulations! You Have Won Russian Roulette

Alternative Paths

Imagine you arrange to meet a Russian oligarch outside of your city in the forest nearby. He arrives shortly thereafter carrying both a suitcase and gun; placing his suitcase on the hood of his car so you can see its contents: $10 million total in stacks of cash! When asked by him whether you would like to play Russian roulette he suggests this strategy by inviting you to pull one trigger to win it all - one bullet with five chambers currently empty would make all this yours in just one pull of a trigger pull! You consider all possible outcomes: $10 million would change everything; never having to work again or moving from stamp collecting stamp collecting stamp collecting stamp collecting stamp collecting stamp collecting stamp collecting stamp collecting to collecting sports car collecting!

Accepting the challenge, you put the revolver to your temple and squeezed the trigger, hearing an audible click before feeling adrenaline rush through your body - but nothing happened; the chamber was empty! Now with money in hand, you move to one of the most picturesque cities you know where they will likely build luxurious villas that cause upset among local residents.

One of your neighbours whose home now lies nearby is an accomplished lawyer, working twelve-hour days over 300 weeks a year at rates not uncommonly impressive for lawyers: $500 an hour. His net yearly savings, after taxes and living expenses, amount to half a million after all expenses have been taken into consideration. You smile inwardly whenever he passes by in your driveway: it will take him twenty years just to catch up with you!

Imagine this: after 20 years, your hardworking neighbor has managed to amass $10 million. A journalist comes along one day and writes an article on more affluent residents in your area - featuring photos of spectacular buildings and second wives that you and your neighbour have acquired, interior design features and exquisite landscaping details; but one key difference remains hidden from view: risk that lurks behind each of their $10 Million accounts; for this piece to make sense, they would need to recognize alternative paths available to each.

But it is not only journalists who fall short with this skill - we all are.
Alternative paths refer to all the outcomes that could have occurred but did not. When playing Russian roulette, four possible paths lead to winning $10 million while five others could lead to your death - making for a stark difference. By contrast, for lawyers practicing law, their possible paths tend to lie closer together; earning $200 an hour in rural settings; but

in urban New York working for one of the major investment banks could net them $600 an hour without risking an alternate path that might have cost them their fortune or life.

Alternative paths may not always be visible, and we rarely consider them. Yet those who speculate in junk bonds, options, and credit default swaps to make millions should keep in mind the many alternative routes leading straight towards ruin. A rational mind would argue that the value of 10 million earned through riskier means would be less than that earned through more mundane work (though an accountant may disagree).

Recently, I attended a dinner with an American friend who proposed we toss a coin to see who should pay the bill. Unfortunately for him, he lost and so this awkward situation became more troublesome for me when he was my guest in Switzerland. "Next time around," I promised, 'whether here or back home in New York I will cover half the tab myself." He thought about this and told me, 'Considering alternative paths you may have already paid half.'

Conclusion: Risk can often be invisible, so always assess possible alternative paths before making decisions involving risky dealings. While success attained through such risky means may seem attractive at first, to a rational mind it should not compare with success achieved via more laborious means (for instance by becoming a lawyer, dentist, ski instructor, pilot, hairdresser or consultant). While viewing other paths from an external viewpoint is challenging; looking inside yourself is almost impossible as your brain will work overtime convincing you of its worth despite any perceived risks involved and will actively block out thoughts of taking paths other than those being considered at present.

See also Black Swan (ch. 75); Ambiguity Aversion (ch. 80), Fear of Regret (ch. 82) and Self-Selection Bias (ch. 47)

FALSE PROPHETS

FORECAST ILLUSION

Everyday experts bombard us with predictions, but how reliable are they really? Up until recently no one bothered to investigate; but then came Philip Tetlock. Over a 10-year period he evaluated 28,361 predictions from 284 self-appointed professionals; his results indicated only marginal improvement over random forecasting generators in terms of accuracy; media darlings were particularly poor performers while prophets of doom such as those that predicted the collapse of Canada, Nigeria, China, India, Indonesia South Africa Belgium or even the E.U. None have imploded!

John Kenneth Galbraith famously stated, 'There are only two kinds of forecasters: those who know nothing and those who do not realize they know nothing,' earning himself widespread criticism in his profession. Fund manager Peter Lynch further summarised it eloquently: 'In America there are approximately 60,000 economists employed full-time attempting to forecast recessions and interest rates; had they done this twice successfully, they'd all be millionaires by now; yet most remain gainfully employed which tells us something. This was published ten years ago - today this number could triple without effect on quality forecasting whatsoever!

Problematic is that experts enjoy unrestricted discretion with little repercussion. If an expert breaks an expectation or violates regulations, their actions could have serious repercussions that are difficult to manage and manage effectively.
When they get it right, experts reap publicity, consultancy offers and publication deals; when they miss it completely, no penalties - financial or reputational - apply. This incentive motivates them to churn out as many prophecies as they possibly can; indeed, the more forecasts they generate coincidentally come true! Ideally, experts should pay into some sort of forecast fund - such as $1000 per prediction; should their forecast come true, they get back their investment plus interest while any money lost due to inaccurate predictions goes towards charity instead.

So what exactly can be predicted and what cannot? Some things are fairly easy to predict; I know approximately how much weight I will weigh next year. However, as complexity and timeframe increase, so too will our ability to predict its future - this includes global warming, oil prices or exchange rates; inventions are equally unknowable - had we known what technologies we would invent in future we would already have created them.

Be skeptical when encountering predictions. I always take care to smile whenever I hear one and then pose two questions to myself about any predictions made by experts: 1) what incentive do they have to keep making incorrect predictions? and 2) if an expert works as an employee could he risk his job if his predictions keep failing? Are they paid consultants with credentials in books and lectures, or self-appointed gurus who make a living through self-publishing or public lectures? Those reliant on media attention tend to make predictions with shocking prophecies that often go unreported by media outlets. Second, what has been their success rate over five years - how many predictions has the forecaster made and how many were successful versus which weren't correct - this information should never go unreported by media outlets so please do not publish forecasts without providing track records from pundits.

Tony Blair once stated it this way: 'I don't make predictions; never have, never will.
See also Expectations (ch. 62); Planning Fallacy (ch. 91); Authority Bias (ch. 9); Hindsight Bias (ch. 14); Overconfidence Effect (ch. 15); Illusion of Control (ch. 17); Hedonic Treadmill (ch. 46) and Black Swans (ch. 75)

Chris is 35. He studied social philosophy as a teenager and developed an interest in developing countries since. Following graduation, Chris worked two years with the Red Cross in West Africa before returning to its Geneva headquarters as the head of its African aid department for three more years before eventually earning an MBA and writing his thesis on corporate social responsibility. Now it appears likely either A) Chris works for one of the major banks where he also oversees its Third World foundation or B). Which scenario seems most probable?

Most people tend to select option B, however this is the incorrect response. B says both that Chris works for a major bank as well as that an additional condition has been met - employees working within a bank's Third World foundation comprise a small subset of bankers; option A would therefore be more likely. Nobel laureates Daniel Kahneman and Amos Tversky have extensively studied this phenomenon.

As humans, we're drawn to narratives that seem pleasing or plausible; stories about Chris the aid worker that are persuasive or convincing increase the risk of false reasoning. If I had put this question differently you might have recognised all these extra details as excessive; perhaps for example: 'Chris is 35 and works at either A) a bank in New York with an office on the twenty-fourth floor overlooking Central Park or B) neither'

Again, take an example from Seattle airport closure and flight cancellation: which scenario is most likely? In this instance, A is more likely since B implies an extra condition has been met: bad weather. Considering other possibilities could also close it such as bomb threats, accidents or strikes; but most likely we do not consider such matters when considering plausible stories like A or B. Now that you understand this process better, do it with friends to see which outcome most prefer!
Even experts can fall victim to the conjunction fallacy. At an international conference for future research in 1982, experts - all academics - were divided into two groups at an event organized by Daniel Kahneman: group A received his forecast that oil consumption will decrease by 30%; group B heard it as "A dramatic rise in oil prices will cause consumption to decrease by 30%". Both groups then had to indicate how likely each scenario seemed; it quickly became evident that group B felt much stronger about its forecast than did group A.

Kahneman believes in two types of thinking. One type is intuitive, automatic and direct; the second conscious, rational, slow, laborious and logical. Unfortunately, intuitive thinking draws conclusions long before conscious mind does; I personally experienced this after the 9/11 World Trade Center attacks when looking for travel insurance policies with special 'terrorism cover' added. Even though other policies covered all possible incidents including terrorist acts (but I fell for their offer anyway!). What made it even more ridiculous was my willingness to pay more for what seemed an attractive yet unnecessary add-on!

Conclusion: Don't confuse left and right brains; intuitive and conscious thinking differ significantly more. When making important decisions, keep this distinction in mind when making important choices: subconsciously we tend to prefer plausible stories; look out for convenient details and happy endings that seem plausible to you, rather than those that require additional conditions to meet. Remember: additional conditions will reduce rather than increase likelihood.

See also Base-Rate Neglect (ch. 28); Story Bias (ch. 13) 42

Consider these two statements when framing:

"Hey, the garbage can is overflowing!"

"It would be really wonderful if you could empty the trash, honey."

Tonality makes music: what matters is how a message is communicated; differently communicated messages will also be received differently by their recipients - this technique known as framing in psychological parlance.

Kahneman and Tversky conducted an experiment in the 1980s in which they presented two options for an epidemic-control strategy; their participants were told that 600 lives were at stake with either option A or option B saving 200 of them. Option B offered only a 33% chance that all 600 individuals would survive and 66% likelihood that no one would make it out alive, with 200 survivors expected to make it through both scenarios; most respondents chose option A over B due to its larger chance of survival - believing in the wisdom that having something tangible is better than losing out later. Reframing the same options became extremely fascinating: "Option A kills 400 people", while "Option B offers a 33% chance that no one will die and a 66% chance all 600 will die". At that point, only a minority chose A and most picked B; researchers noted a remarkable U-turn among almost all participants; depending on whether phrasing (survive or die) changed decision making completely.

One example: Researchers presented a group of people with two kinds of meat labelled as being 99% fat free and 1% fat, then asked them which was healthier. Can you guess which they chose? You guessed right - respondents chose the first option regardless of its higher fat content!

Glossing is an increasingly popular form of framing. According to its rules, a falling share price becomes the subject of correction while an overpaid acquisition price becomes "goodwill".
Every management course magically turns problems into opportunities or challenges; being fired becomes an opportunity to 'reassess my career' or dealing with fallen soldiers is seen as a chance to create opportunities or address challenges.

Death on the battlefield becomes the equivalent of war hero status; regardless of its cause or manner. Genocide becomes "ethnic cleansing", while emergency landings, for instance on Hudson River, are celebrated as triumphs of aviation (although certainly a textbook landing would count even more as such triumphs!). A successful emergency landing, for instance on

Hudson River is widely celebrated as such an achievement (shouldn't an airport runway count as even greater triumph of aviation?)

Have you ever taken a closer look at ETF (exchange-traded funds) prospectuses and brochures? Usually the brochure illustrates recent performance statistics with just enough historical detail to create an appealing upward curve, which is known as framing. A simple piece of bread may serve as another great example - depending on its representation as either symbolic or actual body of Christ can create discord within religion as seen during the 16th Century Reformation period.

Framing can also be employed effectively in commerce. Take used car salesmen: their message leads consumers to focus on only certain factors when considering purchasing them, whether through salesman-delivered messages, signs touting specific features or their own criteria. For instance, when viewing used cars with low mileage and good tyres as selling points - often without regard to engine state, brake condition, interior state etc - and focus more heavily on mileage/tyres than any other aspects. Unfortunately it can be difficult taking in all possible pros/cons when making our purchasing decisions; had other frames been used when selling the car we might have made different choices than we did.

Authors are masterful framers. A crime novel would quickly become tedious if all of its pages simply showed each murder as it happened - "stab by stab". Even as we gradually discover motives and murder weapons, framing adds drama and suspense into the story.

Conclusion: Be conscious that any communication contains some degree of framing; every fact, whether provided by trusted friends or published in credible newspapers, can also be affected by framing effects - even this chapter's contents!

See also Contrast Effect (ch. 10); Contrast Aversion (ch. 21); Fear of Regret (ch. 82); Loss Aversion (ch. 32); Reciprocity (ch. 6); The Anchor Effect (ch. 30) and Sleeper Effect (ch. 70).

WATCHING AND WAITING IS PAINFUL

Action Bias

In soccer penalty situations, it takes less than 0.3 seconds for the ball to travel from its original kicker to the goalkeeper; thus limiting his time for watching its trajectory before making his decision on when it must be kicked back out again. Soccer players taking penalty kicks tend to aim their shots one third of the time at the middle, one third to either side and a third off-center of their goals, which hasn't gone unnoticed by goalkeepers who dive either left or right depending on where players shoot from. Rarely do players remain standing in the center, even though approximately one-third of all balls land there. Why would they risk saving penalties by not standing? Simply because it makes for better television; appearance plays an important part. Dive to one side rather than freezing on spot may look more impressive and feel less embarrassing; that is called action bias: looking active even though nothing concrete results from it.

This research comes from Israeli researcher Michael Bar-Eli, who conducted extensive tests of penalty shoot-outs. Not just goalkeepers are susceptible to action bias - imagine if a group of youths emerges from a nightclub and begin shouting and gesturing at each other before becoming contentious and becoming embroiled in arguments among themselves. Situation teetering on the brink of full-scale violence, young and senior police officers alike remain on standby, monitoring from a distance until casualties emerge and intervening when needed. If this situation were left in the hands of young, inexperienced officers alone, it can quickly turn violent; young, eager officers succumbing to action bias may react immediately and rush in head first, often leading to casualties as a result. According to research findings, later intervention facilitated by senior officers can result in reduced casualties.

Action bias is amplified when confronted with something unfamiliar or unclear. At first, many investors behave similarly to young, overeager police officers outside a nightclub: their inexperience means they cannot assess the stock market so they compensate with hyperactivity; unfortunately this wastes precious time; Charlie Munger famously summarized this approach by saying 'We need discipline in avoiding doing any damn thing just because inactivity becomes unbearable.'

Action bias exists even among highly educated circles. When an illness strikes a patient, even doctors with advanced degrees often respond negatively and delay in seeking appropriate medical treatments for them.
As soon as a condition cannot be properly diagnosed and doctors must choose between intervening (i.e. prescribing something) or waiting and seeing, their decisions to intervene tend towards taking immediate action rather than sitting and waiting until something

definitive happens. Such decisions do not reflect profiteering but instead represent human tendencies to take action rather than remaining dormant when faced with uncertainty.

So what's driving this tendency? In our former hunter-gatherer environment (which suited us perfectly), actions trumped reflection. Lightning-fast reactions were essential for survival; deliberation could prove fatal. When our ancestors saw something at the edge of the forest that looked similar to a sabre-tooth tiger silhouettes they quickly took action; rather than contemplate whether something may have been there they simply made for safety, running quickly away rather than dwelling upon potential threats for too long - unlike us today where our instincts may tell us otherwise.

Though our society increasingly recognizes contemplation as valuable, outright inaction remains a cardinal sin. If you make the correct decision by waiting, no medal or statue with your name on it awaits you; on the contrary, demonstrating decisiveness and quick judgment when things improve can bring accolades from employers, statesmen or even mayors; rash actions tend to win more often in society at large than prudent wait-and-see strategies.

Conclusion: when confronted by new or uncertain circumstances, our instinct may be to do something, anything - no matter the consequences - just so as not to feel helpless or upset. Unfortunately, this tendency often backfires by leading us down paths that worsen things rather than improving them. While waiting may not make headlines in itself, if a situation remains unclear it might be wiser to sit on your hands until a clearer assessment can be done of your options; according to Blaise Pascal 'all human problems stem from man being unable to sit quietly in one room alone' in his study at home.
See also Omission Bias (ch. 44); Overthinking (ch. 90); Procrastination (ch. 85); It Will Get Worse Before It Gets Better Fallacy (ch. 12); and an Inability to Close Doors (Ch 68) as possible factors of mishandled communication issues.

Why Are YOU the Solution, Or Part of the Problem?

Omission Bias

Imagine being on a glacier with two climbers. One slips and falls into a crevasse; calling for help may have saved him, but you don't - instead pushing them both into ravines where they both die quickly afterwards - which one's death weighs on your conscience more?

Rational consideration reveals both options are equally repugnant, leading to death for your companions. Yet something makes us rate the passive option more favorably; this phenomenon is known as the Omission Bias and occurs where both actions and inaction lead to fatal outcomes; we tend to prefer inaction because its results seem less disturbing.

Imagine you are the head of the Federal Drug Administration, and must decide whether or not to approve a drug for terminally ill patients with potentially deadly side effects - these pills have killed 20% immediately while saving lives of 80% more over a short time frame. What would your decision be?

Most would be likely to deny approval; to them, passing through a drug that kills one out of every five patients seems far worse than failing to administer its cure to the other 80%. Such decisions illustrate perfectly the omission bias. Imagine becoming aware of such bias but opting to approve anyway in the name of reason and decency, only for when one of your patients dies an outrage ensues and you find yourself without work! As civil servants or politicians it would be wiser - indeed essential - for them - taking seriously this pervasive form of bias while even encouraging it further!

Case Law shows the depth of such "moral distortion". Euthanasia, even when desired by those dying, is illegal while deliberate refusal of life-saving measures (for instance following DNR orders - Do Not Resuscitate orders) remains legal.

Such reasoning explains why so many parents believe it to be completely acceptable not to vaccinate their children, even though vaccination has been proven to substantially lower risks associated with disease transmission.
Though vaccination carries with it some very small risk of adverse side effects, overall vaccination makes sense; not only for individuals' own sakes but for society as a whole - immune individuals cannot infect other people with their illness and in turn spread it further. Of course if non-vaccinated children contracted any sickness they might accuse their parents of harming them by refusing vaccination - yet this would seem less serious than if they intentionally infected their kids themselves!

Omission bias lies at the root of delusions: We prefer waiting until other people do it instead of taking steps ourselves to act upon it. Investors and business journalists are more forgiving towards companies that produce no new products than against those producing subpar ones, even though both paths lead to ruin. Sitting passively on miserable shares feels better than actively buying bad ones; building no emission filters into coal plants seems superior to taking steps such as removing one for cost reasons; failing to insulate homes seems preferable to burning all that extra fuel; failing to declare income tax is less untoward than filing false tax documents, even though both paths lead to state losses either way.

We explored action bias in Chapter 7. However, is it the opposite of omission bias? Not exactly; action bias leads us to compensate for lack of clarity with futile hyperactivity when things seem unclear or contradictory; while omission bias often manifests where information is easily discernible: an insight might reveal future misfortune that we could avoid through direct action but this insight doesn't generate as much motivation in us to take a stand against it.

Omission bias can be hard to spot; action are usually more noticeable than inaction. Student movements from the 1960s coined an effective slogan against it: 'If you are not part of the solution, then you are part of the problem.'

Notes on Volunteer Error (Ch. 65); Action Bias (Ch. 43); Procrastination (Ch 85).

DON'T BLAME ME

Self-Serving Bias

Do you regularly read annual reports, with special focus on what the CEO has said? If not, that is unfortunate as there you can find numerous examples of an error which all too often comes into play - self-serving bias. Whenever the company experiences success, the CEO takes time to highlight all their efforts - such as making smart decisions, tireless work and cultivating an innovative corporate culture. If a company has had an unsuccessful year, we read about a variety of factors that contributed to its decline: exchange rate fluctuations, government interventions, Chinese trade practices that violate Western intellectual property standards, hidden tariffs that reduce consumer trust etc. In short: our minds attribute success and failures externally rather than internally - this is self-serving bias at work!

Even if you never heard the term, high school taught many a student the meaning of self-serving bias. If they earned an A, their success reflected solely upon them whereas failure meant unfair testing procedures were used by administrators and educators.

But grades don't seem to matter anymore: maybe the stock market has taken their place. When your portfolio makes a profit, you applaud yourself; when it performs poorly, blame is placed squarely with "the market" (whatever this implies) or perhaps that annoying investment adviser. I myself am an adept user of self-serving bias: when my new novel skyrockets to bestseller list status I celebrate it as my best book yet; if it flops amid new releases it must mean readers simply aren't recognising it or critics being jealous that have something against me that doesn't recognize good literature in my books!

Researchers conducted a personality test and randomly allocated participants high or low scores; those receiving high marks found it thorough and fair; those receiving low marks found it completely useless. Why do we attribute success to ourselves and failure elsewhere? There are various theories, with perhaps one simple explanation being this: it feels good! Furthermore, evolution would likely have addressed it much earlier.
Over a hundred thousand years, self-serving bias was eradicated as human society advanced, but in our modern world with many hidden risks it may reemerge and quickly lead to catastrophe. Richard Fuld, often referred to as the self-proclaimed 'master of the universe' could well endorse this view; after being CEO at Lehman Brothers until its bankruptcy filing in 2008 he may well still claim this title while blaming government action as the cause.

Students taking SAT tests typically score between 200 and 800 points. When asked a year later to update their scores, many tend to increase them by roughly 50 points - without ever lying or exaggerating the numbers, simply "enhancing" it until they come to believe the new number themselves.

My building houses an apartment shared by five students, whom I frequently see in the elevator. One said he took out his trash every second or third time; another: every third or fourth time; while Roommate #3 claimed to do it roughly 90% of the time! Their answers should have added up to 100%, but instead totalled an impressive 320%! Each boy overestimated their roles - something all humans tend to do. Studies have also demonstrated this phenomenon among married couples where each assumes they contribute over 50% toward marriage health.

So how can we overcome self-serving bias? Do you have friends who tell the truth without any holds barred? If that's the case for you, count yourself lucky. If not, bring in at least one enemy for coffee and ask their honest opinion of your strengths and weaknesses; you will always be thankful you did it!

See also Hindsight Bias (ch. 14); Overconfidence Effect (ch. 15); Not-Invented-Here Syndrome (ch. 74); Survivorship Bias (ch. 1), Beginner's Luck (ch 49) Cognitive Dissonance (Ch 50); Forer Effect (Ch 64); Introspection Ilusion (Ch 67) and Cherry-Picking (Ch 96) to become familiar with.

WATCH WHATEVER YOU WISH FOR!

Hedonic Treadmill

Imagine one day the phone rings and an enthusiastic voice tells you that you have won a lottery jackpot of $10 Million! How would that make you feel, and for how long would it last? Or another scenario may play out: someone calls to inform you of their loss of a best friend; again how would you react and for how long would the effects last?

In Chapter 40, we examined the low accuracy of predictions in various fields such as politics, economics and social events. We came to the conclusion that self-appointed experts are no better than random forecast generators at providing accurate predictions. Now let us move onto another area: How accurately can we predict our feelings? Are we experts on ourselves? Would winning the lottery make us happier for years to come? Harvard psychologist Dan Gilbert suggests otherwise; his studies of lottery winners indicate that any positive effect quickly dissipated within months, leaving people as content or discontented as before after receiving their cheque - this phenomenon he refers to as 'affective forecasting; our inability to correctly predict our own emotions.

One banking executive decided to build himself a new home outside the city with his ample income, dreaming of creating a villa featuring ten rooms, swimming pool and stunning lake and mountain views. His plan became reality. Within weeks of his purchase, he beamed with excitement. Unfortunately, that enthusiasm soon vanished and six months later he was more miserable than ever. Why had this happened? Well, research shows us that happiness quickly dissipates after just a few months, leaving the villa no longer representing his dreams; coming home each day to an unwelcome reality: opening its door and not knowing where it led him... Poor guy: his feelings toward the villa were indifferent compared to how they felt about his one-room student apartment. Additionally, they now faced two one-hour commutes per day! Studies reveal that driving can be an immense source of discontent and stress, and that most people never get used to the experience. Therefore, those without natural affinity for commuting will likely endure two long commutes each day (at minimum). Therefore, my friend's dream villa had an overall negative effect on her happiness.

Many others do not fare any better: individuals who alter or advance in their career often suffer a similar fate.
Scientists refer to this phenomenon as the hedonic treadmill: we work hard, advance financially and gain more wealth - yet none of this makes us any happier.

So how do negative events such as spinal cord injuries and friend losses impact us? Typically, we overestimate their duration and intensity - for instance when relationships end it can seem as though life will never be the same but within three or so months they have returned to dating and finding happiness once more.

Wouldn't it be wonderful if we knew exactly how happy a new car, career or relationship will make us? Luckily this is something we can measure in part. Take these scientifically sound guidelines as your guides when making better, brighter decisions: 1) Avoid negative things you cannot adapt to over time, such as commuting, noise pollution or chronic stress. 2) Do not place too much reliance on material goods such as cars, houses, lottery winnings, bonuses or prizes as sources of long-term happiness. 3) Seek as much freedom and autonomy as possible since lasting positive changes often stem from taking positive actions on one's own initiative. Pursue your passions even if it means foregoing some income; invest in friendships; most people find lasting happiness through professional status as long as it does not change peer groups at once - in other words, if you ascend to CEO role while only fraternising with other executives, the effect quickly diminishes.

Forecast Illusion (Ch. 40); Neomania (Ch. 69) and Envy (Ch. 86) should all be seen as danger signs and should not be treated lightly.

WE ALL SHOULD REMEMBER NOT TO MARVEL AT OUR OWN EXISTENCE AND LIVE ACCORDINGLY!

As I traveled from Philadelphia to New York, I became stuck in a traffic jam. "Why does it always have to be me?", I lamented, while gazing upon southbound drivers racing past at impressive speed on my opposite side. While spending an hour crawling forward at snail's pace with frequent stops for breaking and acceleration, my mind wandered. Was I truly unlucky in life or was this simply my perception? With bank, post office and grocery store lines seemingly picking me out more often than others or were these just simply perceptions?

Imagine that on this highway a traffic jam forms 10% of the time; my chances of getting stuck is not greater than its likelihood, but my likelihood of becoming stuck at any one point on my journey exceeds this figure due to being limited in my forward movement during such situations; furthermore, once one arises and I become stuck, it becomes much more noticeable to me than had it stayed moving at its normal rate.

Similar logic applies to bank counters or traffic lights: on an average journey between A and B with 10 traffic lights, one will always be red while the rest green; however, you could spend over 10% of your travel time waiting at red lights - although this might not seem right; imagine travelling at near the speed of light: you would likely spend 99.99% (not 10%) of time waiting and cursing red traffic lights!

As soon as we complain of bad luck, it's wise to be wary of self-selection bias. When my male friends gripe about lack of women in their companies and female friends complain about too few men, this has nothing to do with bad luck - these grumblers form part of a sample which shows the likelihood that most male workers work in industries dominated by mostly men (or vice versa for female workers). Furthermore, living in countries like China or Russia with large proportions of either gender means you might become part of that larger group and feel hard done by. When voting occurs during elections, this phenomenon becomes most apparent;
At voting time, it is highly likely that your vote corresponds with the winning majority's majority vote.

Marketers frequently fall prey to self-selection bias. Marketers can fall into it through marketing surveys that attempt to assess customer value of their newsletter, but only reach current subscribers who are fully satisfied, have time and have not cancelled. Thus, these polls prove ineffectual.

Remarks made by my rather saddening friend recently touched upon a common self-selection bias; only living beings can make such observations; nonentities often don't give much thought to their nonexistence. Yet this same delusion forms the basis of many philosophical works as they marvel year-after-year at language's development; I sympathize with their amazement but find their amazement unjustifiable; language would simply not exist without us to revere its miracle; its wonder only becomes tangible by being exposed to its surroundings - its miracle only become tangible by way of its existence in its environment - like its miracle of creation or destruction by human minds!

Amusing is this recent telephone survey: A company conducted it to ascertain, on average, how many phones (landline and cell) each household owned. They were amazed to find out that no household claimed to have none! Truly an astonishing achievement.

See also Alternative Paths (ch. 39); Feature-Positive Effect (ch. 95); Swimmer's Body Illusion (ch. 2) for further discussion.

ASSOCIATION BIAS

Kevin has made three presentations of his division's results to the company's board and each time, everything went flawlessly - and Kevin believes this green polka-dot boxer shorts to be his lucky underpants!

Kevin couldn't resist buying the stunning engagement ring she showed him; although, at $10,000 it was well over his budget for second marriage, something about this woman made it irresistible to him; perhaps associating this beautiful object with someone would inspire hope for future brides that she might also be breathtakingly beautiful?

Each year, Kevin visits his doctor for a check-up and is usually told that, at 44 years old, his health is in good shape. Twice however he has left with alarming news: once for his appendix (which was swiftly removed); and another for an initially swollen prostate which, upon further inspection turned out to be mere inflammation rather than cancer - both times Kevin left feeling worried and both days being extraordinarily hot; since then whenever temperatures begin rising around one of his check-up appointments he promptly cancels it immediately!

Our brains are connection machines. For example, when we consume an unknown fruit and experience nausea afterward, our minds create knowledge. However, this method also creates false knowledge. Russian scientist Ivan Pavlov was the first to study this phenomenon using bells to measure salivation in dogs; later however, just the sound alone would cause salivation; creating links between two seemingly unrelated functions like bell ringing and saliva production within animal brains - such as sound alone being enough to induce salivation in them.

Pavlov's method applies equally well with humans. Advertising creates links between products and emotions, such as Coca-Cola. As a result, advertisements show happy-faced Coke people who appear together - as opposed to frowning faces or wrinkled bodies that you might see elsewhere in real life. Coke people appear in large clusters compared to real life.

False associations are caused by association bias, which also compromises our decision-making quality. We may associate bearers of bad news with its content automatically (known as shoot-the-messenger syndrome). Some CEOs and investors may consciously or unconsciously avoid hearing negative news - leading to an inaccurate picture of reality. To avoid falling prey to false connections and avoid falling prey to false leads when leading groups of people, instruct your staff members to give only bad news as quickly as possible so as to counteract shoot-the-messenger syndrome - trust that enough positive news will still come your way! To overcome false connections by overcompensating for shoot-the-messenger syndrome by overcompensating with positive messages - overcompensating by overcompensating with good news!

Before email and telemarketing existed, travelling salesmen used door to door sales methods. One day George Foster happened upon a vacant house where an invisible leak had been filling it with gas for weeks - unbeknownst to him, the damaged bell caused a spark when George pressed it which set off an explosion that sent George straight into hospital, although eventually he recovered quickly. Unfortunately though his fear of doorbells lingered so strongly that even years afterward he couldn't go back to work; trying hard as he could only create another emotional attachment which couldn't reverse itself despite knowing this wasn't likely.

Mark Twain captured this important takeaway message beautifully: 'We should glean from every experience only the lessons contained within; lest we become like the cat that sits down on a hot stove-lid and becomes burned - never sitting down again on either hot or cold ones again.'

Be wary when things start off well; take note of Contagion Bias (ch. 54); False Causality (ch. 37); Beginner's Luck (ch 49) as well as Availability Bias and Affect Heuristic. (See chapter 54 for further reading on these subjects).

WATCH OUT WHEN THINGS START TO HAPPEN FAST

BEGINNER'S LUCK

We recently explored association bias, or our tendency to see connections where none exist. For example, regardless of all of Kevin's success with big presentations while wearing green polka-dot underpants, they cannot guarantee him success every time.

Now we come to one of the more tricky forms of association bias: creating an artificial link with the past. Casino players know this tactic well: they call it beginner's luck. People new to a game who lose in their initial rounds often wisely fold, while whoever strikes lucky tends to continue. When first timers strike lucky however, their confidence may lead them to increase stakes even further - only for them to find out later that probabilities have returned back to average levels soon after!

Beginner's luck plays an essential role in economic success. Imagine company A, which acquires smaller companies B, C and D successively without incident and successfully completes each acquisition - building their confidence as each merger proves too challenging to manage and estimated synergies impossible to realise despite objective evidence pointing in this direction from previous acquisitions - only for beginner's luck to blind them from this reality.

Similar trends occurred with the stock exchange. Drawn to its initial success, many investors poured their life savings and even loans into Internet stocks during the late 90s - unaware that their remarkable profits at that time weren't due to any knowledge-based stock-picking abilities but simply an upward market trend; even those without any prior investing knowledge often enjoyed massive wins when things finally turned downward. When that momentum finally faded away however, many were left facing mountains of dot-com debt.

As was seen during the recent U.S. housing boom, many individuals fell for this trap: dentists, lawyers, teachers and taxi drivers abandoned their careers to 'flip' houses for profit - buying them at bargain basement prices and then immediately selling them back at higher prices - leading them down an intoxicating path toward fat profits but actually with little relevance to real life or their careers.
Housing boom allowed even amateur brokers to prosper; investors took on huge debt as they purchased more and larger mansions, and when the bubble eventually burst they were left with only unsellable properties as assets.

History provides us with ample evidence of novice's luck: neither Napoleon nor Hitler would have embarked on campaigns against Russia without previous victories in smaller battles to back them up.

But how can one distinguish beginner's luck from real talent? While there is no set rule to help make that determination, two tips may prove effective: firstly, if your performance consistently outshines that of others over an extended period, talent likely plays a part. Second, when there are more competitors competing for your business, chances increase of someone striking it big and taking market leadership for multiple years - possibly you! When that occurs among ten competitors, be proud to celebrate yourself as market leader! However, being among the top players (in financial markets) can be seen as evidence of talent; but if you find yourself top dog among 10 million players in one particular year - which could happen easily enough with all sorts of players participating - don't start visualising an empire like Buffett just yet; chances are likely you have just been lucky!

Watch and wait before drawing any definitive conclusions. Beginner's luck can be devastating; to protect against misconceptions and disprove theories as an effective scientist would, I sent my novel Thirty-five out to one publisher where it was immediately accepted; for a moment it felt like genius success (the odds that this publisher would take it on were 1/15,000. To test my theory further I then sent out copies to 10 additional big publishers... and received 10 rejection letters back bringing my notion quickly back down to earth.

See also: Survivorship Bias (ch. 1); Self-Serving Bias (ch. 45); Association Bias (ch. 48); False Causality (ch. 37); Illusion of Skill (ch. 94)

SWEET LITTLE LIES

COGNITIVE DISSONANCE

A fox crept slowly up to a vine and gazed longingly upon its abundant, purple grapes. He placed his front paws against its trunk, stretched his neck out, and tried to reach for them but they were too high up. Irritated, he gave another attempt - his jaw snapped only at air. Finally he leapt with all his strength only to land back down again on earth with an audible thud; not even one leaf had moved. Holding his head high, he headed back into the forest - or so thought the fox.

Aesop, the Greek poet, created this fable to highlight one of the most prevalent errors in logic. A discrepancy occurred when the fox set out to do something but failed, creating an inconsistency which can only be resolved one of three ways: A) getting his hands on some grapes somehow B) accepting that his skills may not be sufficient C) admitting his incompetence

C) by retrospectively reinterpreting what has occurred. This approach represents cognitive dissonance or its resolution.

Imagine purchasing a new car only to quickly come to regret your choice: its engine sounds like it is taking off and its driver seat uncomfortable. What do you do then? Returning it would be an admission of error and likely would not bring all your money back; so as an alternative approach you might convince yourself that loud engines and uncomfortable seating features are part of its safety features, keeping you from falling asleep behind the wheel; no doubt these smart choices were well thought-out purchases that have brought joyous experiences along with them!

Leon Festinger and Merrill Carlsmith from Stanford University once instructed their students to perform one hour of tedious, monotonous work before dividing them into two groups. Group A members received $1 (it was 1959) as compensation; those in group B received $20; later on they had to disclose how they really found it all--surprisingly enough, those receiving only a dollar found it much more enjoyable and engaging!
Why did they do it? Simply because one measly dollar wasn't enough incentive for them to outright lie; so instead they convinced themselves that the work wasn't that bad; in the same vein that Aesop's fox reinterpreted the situation differently, just like these students. Furthermore, those receiving more had no need to justify what they had done, having already committed a lie while receiving $20 compensation as their fair due. These students experienced no cognitive dissonance.

Imagine applying for a job and losing out to another candidate. Instead of acknowledging that they may have been more qualified for it than you were, you convince yourself that you weren't really interested in taking on that particular role; all along it was just an experiment to see whether your 'market value' could get you an interview invitation.

I recently experienced something similar when faced with choosing between investing in two stocks. The one I selected promptly dropped in value shortly after purchase while shares of another, uninvested one skyrocketed - I simply couldn't bring myself to recognize my mistake! Actually, quite the contrary: I vividly recall convincing a friend that even though the stock was experiencing teething problems, it still had more potential overall. Cognitive dissonance can explain this seemingly irrational reaction. As my friend reminded me, the "potential" would have been even greater had I delayed purchasing shares until today. Aesop had warned against that scenario: 'You can try being clever all you want, but eventually you won't reach any grapes."

See also Endowment Effect (ch. 23); Self-Serving Bias (ch. 45); Confirmation Bias (ch. 7-8); "Because Justification" (ch. 52) and Effort Justification (ch. 60).

Hyperbolic Discounting

Have you heard the saying 'Live each day like it were your last.'? It seems to appear at least three times in lifestyle magazines and self-help manuals alike; yet for such an insightful proverb it does nothing for your wits! Imagine what would happen if you followed this advice literally: you would no longer brush your teeth, wash your hair, clean the apartment, turn up for work and pay your bills on time? Without question, in no time at all you would become broke, sick and possibly even behind bars - yet its meaning remains inherently noble; it expresses longing and desire for immediacy which are far too often prioritized above rational thought; to live life to the fullest today without concern about tomorrow is simply not sensible living advice.

Would you rather receive $1,000 over one year or $1,100 over twelve and a month? Most people would likely opt for the latter - with its monthly interest rate of 10% per annum! Plus the extra two weeks' wait could provide great returns, making a wiser decision than waiting too long!

Two more questions. Would you rather receive $1,000 today in cash or wait a month and receive $1,100 more? Most likely, most people would prefer cash today; yet this is amazing because even waiting one month longer yields $100 extra in both cases; in one scenario it seems obvious enough whereas another one may require patience and consideration before answering accordingly. "What's another year?" you might be asking yourself. Not in this instance; when we introduce "now", however, our brains often make inconsistent decisions and science refers to this phenomenon as hyperbolic discounting. Simply stated, as rewards become closer, our 'emotional interest rate' increases and we become willing to give more up in exchange for them. Unfortunately, most economists still fail to grasp that humans respond inconsistently and subjectively to interest rates; consequently, their models rely on constant interest rates which is highly questionable.

Hyperbolic discounting, or our desire for instantaneous rewards, stems from our animalistic past. Animals would never refuse an immediate reward that might help them attain survival more quickly.
Your rats don't respond well to training; they won't give up one piece of cheese today so as to receive more tomorrow. Yes, squirrels do collect food and save it for later consumption; however, that behavior has nothing to do with impulse control or learning.

And what of children? In the 1960s, Walter Mischel conducted an experiment on delayed gratification that you can find by searching YouTube with "marshmallow experiment". A group of four-year-olds were each given one marshmallow to either consume immediately or wait several minutes and receive another one; unfortunately for most children waiting was impossible; even more impressively however Mischel found that capacity for delayed gratification is an indicator of future career success - thus showing that patience truly is virtue.

With age comes greater self-control, making it easier to postpone rewards. Instead of waiting twelve months to bring home an additional $100, we might gladly wait thirteen if an immediate reward were to arise; such as bank's exorbitant interest rates on credit-card debt or short-term personal loans that prey upon our desire for instant gratification.

Conclusion: Though instantaneous rewards can be very tempting, hyperbolic discounting remains a flaw. When we gain control over our impulses - for instance when drinking alcohol - the better we are at avoiding this trap; otherwise we become vulnerable. On the flipside, if you sell consumer products give customers access to them immediately as some may pay extra just so they don't have to wait, something Amazon takes full advantage of; part of the next-day delivery surcharge goes straight into their coffers! A reminder each week can help avoid this trap -

See Decision Fatigue (Ch. 53); Simple Logic (Ch. 63) and Procrastination (Ch. 85).

Traffic jam between Los Angeles and San Francisco due to surface repairs took thirty minutes of my journey before eventually dissipating into chaos in my rear view mirror - or so I thought. Half an hour later, however, more maintenance work had started up again but strangely enough my level of frustration had decreased greatly because reassuring signs along the road announced: 'We're renovating this highway for you!'

The jam reminded me of an experiment conducted by Harvard psychologist Ellen Langer in the 1970s. For this, she went into a library and waited by a photocopier until a line formed around it before approaching its first user and saying: 'Excuse me, I have five pages to copy; may I use your Xerox machine?' Her success rate was 60%. To increase it to 94% she repeated the experiment while offering a justification: 'Excuse me. I need five copies printed now. May I use your Xerox machine because of time pressure?' In almost every instance she was allowed to proceed. This was understandable: people in a hurry often cut to the front of lines without ever really understanding why. She tried again, this time saying: 'Excuse me, but may I go before you because I need copies?' To her amazement, this proved successful almost always (93%).

Justifying our behavior increases tolerance and helpfulness. Using justification like "because" seems sufficient; no matter if the excuse you give for why they're acting this way is good or not; its just as effective! A sign announcing "We are renovating the highway for you" would only serve to confuse matters; any maintenance crew could just as easily be doing their jobs elsewhere on a highway anyway! Seeing what is going on reassures and calms rather than keeps one unaware. After all, nothing frustrates more than being kept unaware!

At Gate A57 at JFK airport, I waited anxiously for Flight 1234 when the announcement over the loudspeaker stated, 'Attention, passengers. Flight 1234 is currently delayed three hours' I decided to visit the desk to learn why and was back within 15 minutes with no answer or explanation given for its postponement.
I was furious; how dare they leave us waiting in ignorance! Other airlines at least had the decency to inform their passengers: 'Flight 5678 has been delayed by three hours due to operational reasons' -- such a lame excuse would at least provide enough comfort.

People seem obsessed with using the word 'because' even when it isn't necessary; as leaders we have undoubtedly witnessed this trend; without an effective rallying call employee motivation wanes quickly. Simply saying your shoe company exists to produce footwear no longer makes an impressionful case: today higher purposes and stories behind your story must also play a part - such as saying you want your shoes to revolutionise the market (whatever that may mean); providing arch support for better world (or Zappo's claim of being in the happiness business) are all essential parts of making sense of business decisions today if we want success (whatever that means).

If the stock market rises or falls by half a percentage point, market commentators won't offer up any plausible explanation - that it was caused by white noise or an infinite series of market movements. Instead, people want tangible reasons and commentators will select one to blame on; their explanation will often come across as meaningless with frequent references being made to Federal Reserve Bank presidents' pronouncements as culprits.

If anyone asks why you have not completed a task yet, a simple response could be: 'Because I haven't got around to it yet.' Though it might sound ridiculous at first, but this usually does the trick without needing to come up with more plausible reasons for not completing it immediately.

One day I watched as my wife painstakingly separated black laundry from blue. To me it seemed unnecessary since both dark colors are of equal importance, yet this practice has managed to keep my clothing run-free over many years. "Why do you do that?" I inquired of her; to which she replied 'Because I prefer washing them separately". For me that was sufficient explanation.

Never leave home without using "because." This simple but effective word helps smooth human interaction and should be utilized freely.

See also Cognitive Dissonance (Ch. 50); Story Bias (Ch. 13) and Fallacy of the Single Cause (Ch. 97)

DECISION FATIGUE

For weeks, you have been working tirelessly on this presentation. Your PowerPoint slides have been polished to a gleaming sheen; every figure in Excel has been proven accurate; the pitch exemplifies crystal-clear logic. Everything depends on this pitch - if successful, everything depends on it - getting approval from the CEO will mean getting promoted into an executive corner office; otherwise it could result in unemployment benefits being granted or being fired immediately! Your boss's assistant suggests three possible timeslots: 8.00a.m., 11.30a.m. or 6.00p.m - which should it take place?

Psychologe Roy Baumeister and Jean Twenge once filled an entire table with hundreds of inexpensive items ranging from tennis balls and candles to T-shirts, chewing gum, and Coke cans. They then divided their students into two groups; those labeled as decision makers were set apart while those not engaged were labeled non-deciders. He told the first group: 'I will show you sets containing two random items at a time and each time it's up to you to choose between the two choices - at the end of my experiment I will give one of those to you as a souvenir' They believed their decisions would determine which item they kept from each set. He instructed the second group: 'Write down what you think about each item, and I will select one at random to give to you at the end.' Shortly afterwards he instructed each student to put their hand into an ice-cold water source for as long as possible and maintain this position until released. Psychology employs this test as a classic measure of willpower or self-discipline; those lacking willpower will quickly withdraw their hand from the icy water, with decision makers withdrawing faster than non-deciders as their intensive decision-making has sapped their willpower - an effect confirmed in numerous other experiments.

Making decisions can be exhausting. Anyone who has configured their computer online or researched long trips - flights, hotels, activities, restaurants and weather included - knows this all too well: after comparing, considering and choosing, one may feel exhausted after all that comparing, considering and choosing has taken place - science refers to this phenomenon as decision fatigue.

Decision fatigue can be dangerous: as a consumer, you become more susceptible to advertising messages and impulse buys; as an executive-level decision-maker, your ability to make sound judgment calls may decrease considerably.
Willpower can be like a battery: after some time it runs dry and needs charging up. One way of doing this is taking a break to relax and eat something; otherwise willpower will plummet when your blood sugar dips too low; IKEA knows this better than anyone; that is why its

restaurants are conveniently placed throughout its stores, as decision fatigue sets in during your journey through maze-like display areas and towering warehouse shelves and decision fatigue sets in quickly; sacrifice some profit margin for Swedish treats that may help replenish blood sugar before continuing your search for perfect candlesticks before resumed!

Four prisoners in an Israeli jail petitioned the court for early release, starting with Case 1 at 8.50a.m.: an Arab sentenced to 30 months for fraud; Case 2 (scheduled for 1.27p.m.) involves a Jew serving 16 months for assault; Case 3 was set for 3.10p.m.). Case 1 (scheduled for 4.35p.m.) involved a Jew who was given 16 months for assault; Case 4 was an Arab sentenced to 30 months for fraud. How did judges make their decisions? More significant than detainee allegiance or severity was their fatigue in making decisions. The judges granted requests 1 and 2, as their blood sugar levels had not yet returned to normal after breakfast or lunch, yet turned down applications 3 and 4, due to insufficient energy reserves to risk an early release. They took the easy option (the status quo), leaving men in jail. A study of hundreds of verdicts shows that during one session alone, the percentage of 'courageous' decisions gradually drops from 65% to almost none before returning back up after recess - so much for Lady Justice! Still, all is not lost: now you know when best to present your project to your CEO.

See also: Paradox of Choice (ch. 21); Hyperbolic Discounting (ch. 51); Simple Logic (ch. 63) and the Default Effect (ch. 81).

WOULD YOU WEAR HITLER'S SWEATER?

Contagion Bias

Following the fall of Carolingian Empire in France during the ninth century, Europe descended into anarchy. Counts, commanders, knights, and other local rulers frequently engaged in bloody battles; their warriors looted farms, raped women, trampled fields, abducted pastors from church services, captured pastors as hostages and set convents on fire; both church authorities and farmers alike were powerless against these nobles' incessant warring.

In the tenth century, a French bishop came up with an impressive plan. He invited all princes and knights of France to gather in one field while priests, bishops, and abbots collected any relics that they could find around that region to display on display there. At first glance, it was an arresting sight: bones, blood-soaked cloth rags, bricks and tiles all bearing signs of contact between saints. At that time, the bishop, as someone renowned for commanding respect, made an impassioned appeal to nobles present before holy relics to abandon violence against unarmed victims and attacks against unarmed civilians. To emphasize his demands further, he waved bloodied clothes and sacred bones before them as further proof. Nobles must have held such symbols with great reverence; Bishop Gregory's unique appeal to their conscience spread throughout Europe, encouraging 'Peace and Truce of God.' One should never underestimate fear associated with saints during this period or with saint relics according to American historian Philip Daileader.

As an educated person, it may be easy for you to laugh off these superstitions as silly. However, consider this: would you wear something Hitler once wore? Unlikely - perhaps showing that your respect for invisible forces still remains. The sweater no longer embodies any connection to Hitler; there is not one drop of his sweat on it - yet wearing it still brings about feelings of shame and respect for what its author represents. No doubt we wish to project an ideal image to our fellow humans and ourselves alike; yet the thought alone can put us off even when alone and we convince ourselves that touching such clothing doesn't endorse Hitler in any way. Unfortunately, such emotional reactions can be difficult to overcome even among those who consider this topic important - such as politicians. Even people who consider themselves highly rational sometimes struggle to dispel any belief in mysterious forces (me included).

Paul Rozin and his research colleagues at the University of Pennsylvania discovered that mystifying powers can't simply be turned off. Test subjects brought in pictures of their loved ones which they then had to shoot darts at, without harming those depicted; although their hesitation and accuracy compared with regular targets proved far lower - as though some unseen force prevented them from hitting these precious photos.

The contagion bias refers to our inability to disassociate ourselves from certain objects - be they from long ago or more indirectly related (as with photos). My friend worked as a war correspondent for French public television channel France 2. Like passengers on a Caribbean cruise, my friend also collected souvenirs from her adventures - such as straw hats or painted coconuts from each island she visited - as mementoes from each adventure, including one to Baghdad in 2003. Shortly after American troops stormed Saddam Hussein's government palace, she sneaked into his private quarters. Once inside, she quickly noticed six gold-plated wine glasses in the dining area and quickly made off with them. Recently at one of her dinner parties in Paris, the goblets taking pride of place on the dining table caught my attention - one guest asked her if they came from Lafayette; when I mentioned Saddam Hussein to her she casually replied 'no - they are from Saddam. An extremely distressed guest was shocked and began coughing uncontrollably, which forced me to comment: 'Do you realize how many molecules of Saddam's are already part of you by breathing alone? I asked. His cough worsened.

See also Association Bias (ch. 48); Affect Heuristics (ch. 66) for more details.

WHY THERE ISN'T ANY AVERAGE WAR

Imagine taking a bus ride with 49 other people, when at one stop the heaviest person in America boards; at that time, what percentage has increased in average weight among passengers since? Perhaps four per cent? Five? In contrast, at another stop Bill Gates hops aboard; now our focus should not be weight but wealth instead - by how much has wealth increased since four per cent and five respectively? Neither scenario holds!

Let's quickly calculate our second example. Initially, each individual with assets of $54,000 constitutes the statistical middle value, or median. Now add Bill Gates with his fortune estimated to be approximately $59 billion to this mix and watch how quickly the average wealth has increased by more than two million percent to an increase of nearly two billion per cent; rendering any notion of an "average" totally meaningless.

Nassim Taleb advises, in his works on probability theory, not crossing rivers that average four feet deep, due to the risk they impose in crossing them if their depth increases beyond four. Rivers can appear shallow - mere inches - for long stretches before suddenly becoming twenty-foot-deep torrents that threaten your life if crossing. Averages can often mask distributional details - they obscure how values stack up over time.

At an average level, UV exposure on June days does not pose a threat to health. But if you were to spend all summer indoors in an office and then head off to Barbados and lie in the sun without protection for an entire week without using sunscreen - even though overall you were likely receiving less UV light exposure than someone who regularly ventured outside - that would create problems.

All this should be fairly obvious to you already; perhaps even yourself. Say, for instance, you drink one glass of red wine each evening during dinner - that won't pose a health problem and is recommended by many physicians. On December 31, however, if you drink none all year and suddenly consume 356 glasses (the equivalent of sixty bottles), you would likely experience health complications regardless of what the average over the year was.
Update: In today's complex world, distribution is becoming ever more irregular; therefore we will observe Bill Gates-like results across more domains. When it comes to online distribution and website visits, average website visitor counts don't exist: no websites receive equal traffic levels. Mathematicians often refer to this phenomenon as the so-called power law, with certain sites (e.g. New York Times, Facebook or Google) garnering most visits while other pages receive relatively few. Take cities as an example. Tokyo is the only city with an estimated population greater than 30 million on earth, while there are 11 with between 20-30 million, 15 between 10-20 million, 48 between 5-10 million inhabitants, and thousands

between 1-5 million - this distribution follows a power law where some extreme cases dominate overall distributions, leaving no meaningful average figure behind.

What is the average size of a company, population of a city, number of deaths during an average war (in terms of both deaths and duration), Dow Jones daily fluctuation average, cost overrun of construction projects average, how many copies an average book sells per copy sold by publisher; average amount of damage done by hurricane; bonus paid to banker on average; success of marketing campaign averaged for iPhone app downloads and actor salary? You could calculate these answers, but doing so would be fruitless as power law applies here as well.

Take this final example as an illustration: A select few actors earn more than $10 Million annually while thousands and thousands live below the poverty line. Would you advise your child or daughter to enter acting based on an average wage figure that seems acceptable? Probably not - that would be foolish advice.

Conclusion: Before jumping to conclusions based on someone using the term 'average', take a moment and assess its underlying distribution. If anomalous cases (such as Bill Gates' phenomenon) have minimal influence, we may continue to use the concept; but when extreme cases (such as Bill Gates) dominate (like his success with Microsoft), we must disregard its utility altogether and discount the term. Novelist William Gibson advised us all: 'The future is already here - it's just not evenly distributed.'

See also Base-Rate Neglect (ch. 28); Simple Logic (ch. 63); Regression to Mean (ch. 19); Neglect of Probability (ch. 26) and Gambler's Fallacy (ch 29)

BONUSES DESTRUCT MOTIVATION

Motivation Crowding

Recently, my Connecticut friend decided to move to New York City. His move would involve transporting an impressive collection of antiques like rare old books and hand-blown Murano glasses from generations past - I knew how attached he would be to giving these over to a moving company; thus the last time I visited, I offered to carry some of the fragile items myself when returning to Connecticut from NYC. Two weeks later, a thank-you letter arrived with a fifty-dollar bill enclosed!

Switzerland has spent years searching for an appropriate underground repository to store their radioactive waste, with consideration given to several locations including Wolfenschiessen near Berne in central Switzerland. Economist Bruno Frey of the University of Zurich traveled there with colleagues to collect people's opinions at a community meeting; to their amazement, 50.8% supported their proposal! Their positive response can be attributed to various factors: national pride, common decency, social obligation and the prospect of new jobs among others. The team conducted another survey, this time proposing that each townperson accept the proposal if given a hypothetical reward of $5,000 from Swiss taxpayers if they accepted. What resulted? Results decreased dramatically: only 24.6% agreed with it.

Children's daycare centers face similar difficulties: parents collecting their children after closing time. Daycare staff cannot put any remaining kids into taxis or leave them on the kerb until all remaining kids have been collected from school. To discourage parental tardiness, many nurseries have introduced fees for lateness; but studies show this has actually increased tardiness rather than decreasing it. Of course, they could have instituted harsh penalties such as $500 an hour as was offered to each Swiss village resident - but that would miss the point; small yet surprising financial incentives tend to crowd out other forms of incentives which offer much greater returns in terms of returns for everyone involved compared with larger monetary incentives - unlike in this instance.

The three stories illustrate one important truth: money does not always motivate.
At times, money does more harm than good. My friend gave me fifty to make up for his bad deed; instead he undermined it while jeopardising our friendship. Offering compensation to a nuclear repository was seen as bribery by some and lessened patriotic spirit in general; nursery's late fees changed their relationship with parents from personal to monetary, essentially legitimising lateness by parents.

Science has a term for this phenomenon: motivation crowding. When people do something for non-monetary, charitable reasons - out of good deed, so to speak - but payment increases hinder these intentions and any other motivations become diminished by its presence. Financial rewards become the driving force in their actions instead.

Imagine you run a non-profit organisation. Your employees may receive modest wages; yet they are highly motivated because they believe they are making an impactful difference. However, should you decide to implement a bonus system - for instance a small salary increase for every donation secured - motivation will quickly fade as your team shifts focus away from tasks that bring no added reward; creativity, company reputation or knowledge transfer no longer matter - instead, all efforts will focus on soliciting donations as quickly as possible.

So who should be safe from motivation crowding? A quick test may reveal who might be safe from it: do you know any private bankers, insurance agents or auditors who perform their duties with passion and believe in a greater mission? No? Financial incentives and performance bonuses work best in industries with dull jobs; where employees don't care much for the products or companies but simply complete work due to getting a pay cheque. However, start-up owners would do well to harness employee passion as part of promoting the endeavor rather than offering incentives they couldn't pay out anyway.

One last tip for those of you with children: experience has taught us that young people cannot be bought. If you want your kids to do their homework, practice musical instruments or mow the lawn occasionally without your wallet being empty - instead offer a fixed weekly allowance as this will keep them honest without them abusing it and refusing to go to sleep without some form of compensation.

See also Incentive Super-response Tedency (ch. 18); Reciprocity (ch. 6); Social Loafing (ch. 33) for additional discussion of these subjects.

IF YOU DON'T HAVE ANYTHING TO SAY, SAY NOTHING

TWADDLE TENDENCY

When asked by rolling cameras why a fifth of Americans could not locate their country on a world map, Miss Teen South Carolina gave this response in front of rolling cameras: 'I personally believe that U.S. Americans are unable to do so because some people out there in our nation don't have maps; and my belief that our education like South Africa and Iraq should help these countries develop our future as one cohesive global society.' The video went viral.

Catastrophic, you admit it; yet you don't waste too much time listening to beauty queens. Perhaps something like this sentence would suffice: "There is certainly no requirement that this increasingly reflexive transmission of cultural traditions be associated with subject-centred reason and future-oriented historical consciousness. When we become aware of intersubjective constitution of freedom, the possessive-individualist illusion of autonomy disintegrates.""

Remember Jurgen Habermas? He's an outstanding German philosopher and sociologist known for writing Between Facts and Norms.

Both are examples of what's known as the twaddle tendency, where words are used to disguise intellectual laziness, stupidity or underdeveloped ideas. Sometimes it works and sometimes not; for the beauty queen this strategy failed spectacularly while for Habermas it might just work; the more eloquent the language becomes, the easier we fall prey to its allure; when combined with an authority bias it becomes even more dangerous as we accept its message without questioning its truth.

I too have succumbed to the tendency for empty chatter. When I was younger, French philosopher Jacques Derrida captured my imagination; I read his books voraciously but found little clarity from them even after much contemplation and intense analysis. Subsequently his writings took on an almost magical quality which eventually inspired my dissertation topic on philosophy - both tomes were ultimately useless chatter; in ignorance had both become wastes of space in my mind.
Myself into a human, talking smoke machine.

Twaddle in sports can be especially pervasive. Breathless interviewers force equally breathless football players into breaking down every aspect of a game when all they really mean to say is, 'We lost, it's that simple' but presenters need something to fill airtime - and apparently one way they do so effectively is through jabbering away and compelling athletes and coaches to join in; in any event, this kind of rhetoric serves only to mask ignorance and hide ignorance from public view.

Academic environments have also witnessed this phenomenon: when fewer results from any field of science are published, economists become particularly exposed in their comments and forecasts. It holds true in commerce as well: when companies become worse-off financially, their CEO's talking becomes louder - often to cover for hardship or mask difficult circumstances. A notable exception in this regard was former General Electric CEO Jack Welch; during an interview he noted its difficulty: people fear being perceived as simpletons but this actually isn't the case!'

Verbal expression is the mirror of our minds; clear thoughts become statements while vague concepts transform into vague ramblings. Unfortunately, we often lack very lucid thoughts; life is complicated, so understanding just one facet requires considerable mental effort and may take an epiphany for clarity to emerge; until that point arrives it would be wiser to follow Mark Twain's advice that 'If you have nothing to say... say nothing.' Simplicity should not be seen as its beginning but as its destination.

See also Authority Bias (ch.9); Domain Dependence (ch.76); and Chauffeur Knowledge (ch. 16) to gain further insights into this question.

How Can Two States Increase the Average Intelligence Quotient

Imagine yourself running a small private bank that handles the funds of wealthy and mostly retired individuals, such as in Will Rogers Phenomenon
Your two money managers - A and B - report directly to you; Money Manager A handles only ultra-high net-worth individuals while Money Manager B handles wealthier clients but not as extravagantly rich clients as Money Manager A does. Now imagine that the board has asked you to increase both average pools of money within six months so they receive handsome bonuses; otherwise they'll find someone else. Where should you start?

Simple! Just transfer one client with an average managed wealth between A and B to make up the difference, raising both average managed wealth figures simultaneously - without needing to acquire new clients! Once complete, all that remains to decide is: where and how will I spend my bonus.

Imagine changing careers, and taking charge of three hedge funds that invest primarily in privately held companies. Fund A is producing astounding returns while funds B and C struggle. You want to show yourself as the mastermind, so what's your plan? To create the appearance that all three funds have improved significantly without incurring fees for in-house transformation, move a few shares from A over to B or C; pick investments which were negatively affecting A's average returns but could help strengthen B or C; you should see all three funds suddenly become healthier without incurring fees for transformation - people will certainly recognize you for doing it!

This effect is known as stage migration or Will Rogers phenomenon after an American comedian from Oklahoma who famously joked that Oklahomans moving to California raise both states' average IQ. Since most people do not recognise such situations often enough, let us explore this topic further and drill its meaning into your memories.

Consider an auto franchise: you might take charge of two small branches within one town with six salespeople: salesmen numbers 1, 2, 3, 4, 5, and 6 from Branch A are generally more successful at making sales than their counterparts from Branch B. On average, Salesperson 1 tends to sell more.
Each salesman at Branch A sells one car per week; Salesperson 2 shifts two, followed by top salesman No 6 who shifts six each week. By doing the maths, it becomes apparent that Branch A averages two salespeople selling cars each week whereas Branch B leads significantly with five average per salesperson per week! Your decision to transfer salesman number 4 from branch A to branch B results in increased average sales per person at both locations; branch A's average increases from 2.5 units per person to 2.5, while branch B now only comprises two salespeople - numbers 5 and 6, which increase its average sales to 5.5

units per person. Switcheroo strategies don't affect anything overall; rather they create an impressive illusion. Therefore journalists, investors and board members should remain wary when hearing of rising averages across countries, companies, departments, cost centres or product lines.

Medicine provides us with an especially deceiving example of Will Rogers' phenomenon. Tumours are typically divided into four stages; those most treatable fall under Stage I while more aggressive tumors will go through four more steps before reaching Stage IV status - hence giving rise to stage migration as they move along their course. Survival rates for stage-one cancer patients are highest while survival rates for stage-four cancer sufferers are lowest. Every year new procedures come out that enable more accurate diagnoses; screening techniques now reveal even minuscule tumors which no one had noticed previously. As a result, patients previously misdiagnosed as healthy are now counted among stage-one patients and, consequently, average life expectancies have increased for this group of people. Can we consider this an extraordinary medical feat? Unfortunately not; rather stage migration.

See Also: Intention-to-Treat Error (ch. 98); Law of Small Numbers (ch. 61);

Jorge Luis Borges depicts in his short story 'Del Rigidit en La Ciencia' a country in which cartography has reached such sophisticated heights that only the most detailed maps can be used; that is, maps with scale of 1:1 representing their entire country are acceptable. Citizens soon realize, however, that such maps don't offer any real insight and simply repeat information they already possess; an extreme case of information bias - believing more data means better decisions.

As I searched for hotels in Miami recently, I made a shortlist of five potential offers that struck my fancy immediately. One immediately stood out; however, to ensure I found the best value, I kept researching further - reading customer reviews and blog posts, viewing pictures and videos online and going through customer support calls until two hours later, when it became clear which was indeed my ideal hotel: that one which caught my eye at first sight; additional research did not lead me down the right path and instead might as well have resulted in me staying at Four Seasons instead!

Jonathan Baron from the University of Pennsylvania asked physicians this question: a patient presents symptoms which indicate with an 80% likelihood that he or she has disease A; otherwise, the likelihood shifts towards having either disease X or Y instead. As a doctor, how should you choose between these illnesses and treatments that produce similar side effects? Logically, I would suggest selecting Disease A and offering relevant therapy as treatment. Imagine there is a diagnostic test which indicates disease X is present and disease Y detected, but does not accurately reflect actual illness A in all instances; half of the times, its results would show positive and the other half negative. If someone actually does have disease A, however, half of their test results would likely show positive while 50% would display negative. Would you advise conducting the test? Most doctors said yes - even though its results would likely be irrelevant. Even if a positive result occurred from testing, the likelihood that disease A outweighed disease X so no additional information added any real value in terms of decision making.

Medical doctors aren't the only professionals with an appetite for providing additional information.
Managers and investors seem enthralled with information overload. Studies are frequently undertaken when the essential facts are readily available - more data may only serve to waste your time and money, potentially even placing you at a disadvantage. Consider this question: which city has more residents - San Diego or San Antonio? Gerd Gigerenzer of Germany's Max Planck Institute presented this to students from Chicago and Munich universities and 62% guessed correctly: San Diego. Every German student surprisingly answered correctly! Their reasoning? All had heard of San Diego but not necessarily San Antonio; thus choosing

San Diego over San Antonio as being more familiar. On the contrary, Chicagoans had both cities on their mind simultaneously, providing more information and potentially misguiding their answers.

Think about all the economists working for banks, think tanks, hedge funds and governments between 2005 and 2007 who published white papers with numerous forecasts and comments - for banks, think tanks, hedge funds and governments alike - published during that time period - from 2005-2007; all their published white papers; vast library of research reports and mathematical models; formidable reams of comments made; polished PowerPoint presentations made; terabytes of information available via Bloomberg/Reuters news services and worshipping god of information... It all proved meaningless as financial crisis hit global markets - rendering their forecasts and comments meaningless; rendering those forecasts worthless!

Avoid collecting all available data - instead focus on gathering only what's essential. Doing this will enable you to make better decisions; superfluous knowledge is worthless no matter who knows about it - Daniel J. Boorstin said it best: 'the greatest obstacle to discovery is not ignorance but rather the illusion of knowledge'; when confronted by rivals consider killing them with data analysis rather than soft words.

See also Overthinking (ch. 90); News Illusion (ch. 99); Base Rate Neglect (ch. 28) for additional reading.

HURTS SO GOOD

John, a soldier in the U.S. Army, recently completed his paratrooper course and is eagerly awaiting to receive his parachute pin from his superior officer. Finally, at last momentous moment of truth, his superior officer stands in front of him, lines the pin against his chest, pounding so hard against it that it pierced John's flesh causing it to make contact and leave an indent on his skin - ever since then, whenever an opportunity presents itself he opens up his top shirt button to show off its small scar. Decades later all memorabilia except this tiny pin still lives on in a special frame on his living room wall.

Mark had painstakingly restored a rusty Harley-Davidson without assistance, spending every weekend and holiday getting it running while his marriage neared dissolution. Finally, though, after months of work it was road ready and shone brilliantly under the sun's rays. Two years later however, when in desperate need of money Mark sold all his possessions including TV, car and house... but not his prized possession; not even when offered double its actual worth by potential buyers!

John and Mark both suffer from effort justification: when exerting much energy into something, you tend to overvalue its results. John experienced physical pain for his parachute pin; Mark's Harley cost him many hours - nearly his wife! - so much that he values it highly and won't sell it ever.

Effort justification is a classic example of cognitive dissonance. Punching a hole into your chest for something like a merit badge seems absurd. In order to compensate, John's mind overvalues it, elevating its status from something mundane into something semi-sacred. Unfortunately, all this happens unconsciously and is difficult to prevent.

Groups use effort justification to bind members together - for instance through initiation rites. Gangs and fraternities initiate new members by subjecting them to painful or unpleasant tests. Research shows that the more difficult an entrance exam is to pass, the greater pride members take in belonging. MBA schools utilize effort justification similarly: MBA graduates often receive credit for passing rigorous entrance exams into MBA programs.
Students of MBA programs often become exhausted during their study of this qualification; yet when their MBAs have been achieved, many will consider them essential to their careers simply due to the demands put upon them by coursework that was often useless or irrelevant.

An easier form of effort justification is the IKEA effect: furniture we assemble ourselves can seem more valuable than any expensive designer piece, just as hand-knitted socks that we spend hours creating often appear more valuable than any expensive designer item. Even hand-crafted socks may seem hard to part with; tossing away an obsolete pair made with care is difficult. Managers putting long hours of hard work into crafting a strategy proposal may find themselves incapable of appraising objectively; similarly designers, copywriters, product developers or any other professionals who fret over their creations are also guilty.

In the 1950s, instant cake mixes were introduced into the market - which manufacturers believed would be an instant hit among housewives. Unfortunately, housewives took immediate dislike to them, proving the manufacturers wrong.

Reacting to their ease, firms increased the difficulty of food preparation (beating in an egg yourself). This created an enhanced sense of achievement among women who prepared it themselves and increased their appreciation of convenience food products.

Now that you understand effort justification, you can rate projects more objectively. Experiment: whenever you invest a great deal of time and energy in something, take a step back to assess its result - only the result. That novel you spent five years writing that nobody is interested in publishing? Maybe it is not Nobel-worthy after all? And those women you chased for years? Would they accept you more readily if given another shot?

See also: Sunk Cost Fallacy (ch. 5); Cognitive Dissonance (ch. 50)

WHY DO SMALL THINGS SPREAD TOGETHER?, WHY THESE PIECES SHINE BRIGHTLY

Assume you're sitting on the corporate board of a retail company with 1,000 stores; half are located in urban settings while half in rural locales. Your CEO requested a consultant conduct a study on shoplifting; now their findings have been presented. On a wall in front of him were displayed 100 branch names that have experienced high theft rates relative to sales, along with his startling conclusion: 'Branches with higher theft rates tend to be located predominantly in rural areas' After a brief moment of silence and disbelief, the CEO addressed his employees directly: 'After much deliberation and careful consideration, our next steps are clear. Going forward, we will install additional safety systems at all rural branches so we can watch as those hillbillies try to steal from us again. Do we all agree?'

Well...not entirely. After asking the consultant to compile a list of 100 branches with the lowest theft rates, you are surprised when your list includes rural stores! "Location isn't the determining factor," you exclaim with pride as you gaze around the table at your colleagues. 'Size matters; in rural stores a single incident often has an outsized influence on theft rates than larger city branches do - hence why the rates vary more significantly here than with city branches." "Ladies and gentlemen, I introduce you all to the law of small numbers - and it has just caught you off-guard!"

People find the law of small numbers difficult to grasp intuitively, thus journalists, managers and board members often fall for its trap. Let's take an extreme example. Instead of the theft rate we will look at the average weight of employees in each branch. For our example we will consider two stores instead of 1,000: mega-branch with 1,000 employees and mini-branch with two employees; in both stores the average weight corresponds roughly with population average weight (for instance 170 pounds); when hiring or firing personnel does not significantly alter this average. But in small store it will change significantly more significantly due to changes affecting whether their store manager has colleagues that are overweight or lean in weight affecting this average weight significantly more so than large branchs where any hiring or firing decisions by store managers affect its average weight more. In smaller stores cases store managers can affect its average weight by hiring/firing an employee or manager having colleagues either overweight/lean on board (in those instances it affects average weight significantly).

Let's go back to our shoplifting problem for a moment and explore this in more depth. As it turns out, small branches tend to experience greater fluctuations in their theft rates, from very high to extremely low - something no consultant spreadsheet could capture. When listing all theft rates by size - small stores will appear first at the bottom followed by large stores then smaller ones at the top; meaning the CEO's conclusion may have been useless but at least they no longer need an expensive security system at small locations.

Imagine reading in the newspaper: 'Start-ups tend to hire smarter employees. A study by the National Institute of Unnecessary Research calculated the average IQ across American companies; start-ups hired MENSA material!' What would your first reaction be? Hopefully an eyebrow raise. This phenomenon exemplifies how small companies tend to employ fewer workers; thus their average IQs fluctuate more frequently than large corporations, giving small and new businesses high and low scores; the National Institute's study therefore serves no real significance and confirms chance.

Watch out when hearing remarkable statistics regarding any small entities such as businesses, households, cities, data centres, anthills, parishes or schools; what may appear as astounding findings may actually be an innocuous result of random distribution. Nobel Prize winner Daniel Kahneman in his recent book revealed even experienced scientists succumb to this law of small numbers; which can only be considered comforting.

See Also: Exponential Growth (ch. 34);

TAKE CAUTION WHEN HANDLING THIS MATERIAL!

EXPECTATIONS

On 31 January 2006, Google released its financial results for the final quarter of 2005:
revenue increased 97% while net profit surged 82% year over year - a record quarter for
revenue and net profit respectively. As expected, stocks promptly tumbled 16% immediately
upon hearing these incredible numbers; trading had to be suspended and later resumed with
shares dropping 15% more - inducing panicked traders across all trading platforms who
inquired on blogs as to 'what skyscraper is best to jump from? '

What went wrong? Wall Street analysts had anticipated even better results, so when those did
not materialise, $20 billion was subtracted from the media giant's value.

Every investor knows it is impossible to accurately forecast financial results. While one might
expect investors to shrug off poor predictions as "bad guess, my mistake", investors often
react more harshly; as witnessed in January 2006 when Juniper Networks unexpectedly
released earnings per share figures which fell one tenth below analysts' projections; their
share price dropped 21% and company value plummeted $2.5 billion as expectations ran
high leading up to their announcement and any disparity, no matter how slight, was met with
swift punishment from investors.

Many companies strive hard to meet analyst predictions. To escape their fears, some began
publishing earnings guidance estimates; this was a mistake as now the market looks only to
these internal forecasts - which it often analyses more closely - as forecasting tools. CFOs
must achieve these targets exactly; using all accounting techniques at their disposal for
maximum success.

Expectations can also lead to commendable incentives. American psychologist Robert
Rosenthal conducted an eye-opening experiment at various schools. Teachers were informed
of a (fake) new test which could detect students on the verge of experiencing intellectual
growth; so-called 'bloomers'. Twenty per cent of randomly selected students were randomly
classified as high potential; teachers believed these to be high performers.
Rosenthal conducted experiments on students for a year, after which time he discovered that
those students had dramatically higher IQs compared with control group children - this
became known as the Rosenthal Effect (or Pygmalion Effect).

However, unlike CEOs and CFOs who consciously tailor their performance to meet
expectations, teachers' actions were typically unconscious. Unbeknownst to themselves,
teachers may have subconsciously focused more time on bloomers who in turn led to greater
group learning. Furthermore, teachers were so affected by brilliant students that they

attributed not just better grades but also improved personality traits to them - something known as the halo effect.

But how should we respond to personal expectations? One solution is the placebo effect - pills and therapies which seem unlikely to improve health but actually do so anyway. One third of patients registered the effect, though its exact workings remain unknown; all we know for certain is that expectations affect biochemistry within the brain and consequently the whole body - however Alzheimer's patients cannot benefit as their condition impairs an area responsible for handling expectations in the brain.

Expectations may seem intangible, but they have real-world ramifications. Expectations have the power to alter reality and it is impossible to get rid of them entirely; but you can deal with expectations more wisely: raise them for yourself and those close to you in order to increase motivation; while simultaneously lower expectations on things beyond your control such as the stock market. Anticipation can help avoid unpleasant surprises!

See also Black Swan (ch. 75); Forecast Illusion (ch. 40); Halo Effect (ch. 38)

SPEED TRAPS ABOARD!

Simple Logic

Three easy questions. Grab your pen quickly and jot down your answers quickly in the margin. First question: in a department store, both a ping-pong paddle and plastic ball cost $1.10. If one costs one dollar more, how much is the other item? Second question: in a textile factory, five machines take exactly five minutes to produce five shirts; how long will 100 take to produce 100? Thirdly: A pond contains water lilies that multiply exponentially every day, taking up more area each day until completely covering its surface completely (48 days for complete coverage! Don't read further until all answers have been recorded! Don't read further until all answers have been written down! Don't read until after writing down.

Each question contains both an intuitive and an accurate solution; quick, intuitive answers may include 10 cents, 100 minutes and 24 days; however these are incorrect answers and instead require five cents, five minutes, and 47 days as the solution. How many did you answer correctly?

Professor Shane Frederick has created and administered the Cognitive Reflection Test (CRT), with thousands taking it and scoring at least once. So far, students at Massachusetts Institute of Technology (MIT) in Boston have performed best, scoring 2.18 correct answers on average; Princeton University came second with 1.63 while students from University of Michigan scored only 0.83 on average. But average scores in this case don't reveal much: what's interesting are how those who score highly differ from the rest.

Frederick discovered that people with low CRT results tend to opt for the safer choice; something is always better than nothing! While those who scored at least 2 or higher often preferred riskier options like gambling - this was particularly evident among men.

One thing that separates groups is their ability to control impulses. We discussed hyperbolic discounting in detail in Chapter 5, where it discussed the seductive power of "now." Frederick then put to participants this question: 'Would you rather have your desired item now or later on in life?"
"Should I choose between getting $3,400 now or in one month?" is often answered in favor of getting it immediately; those with lower CRT scores tend to make quicker purchasing decisions due to being more impulsive. By contrast, those with high CRT results usually opt to wait several more weeks and exhibit strong willpower to turn away instant gratification - and are rewarded in due time."

Thinking is exhausting; rational consideration requires more willpower than giving into intuition, in other words. Thus Harvard psychologist Amitai Shenhav and his research colleagues conducted an investigation to see how people's CRT results correlated with their religious affiliations; those who scored high were often atheists whereas participants with lower CRT scores believed in God and had divine experiences more often than atheists did - this makes sense as intuitive decision makers tend not to question religious doctrine as rationally.

If your CRT score leaves something to be desired and you want to increase it, start by greeting even simple logic questions with incredulity. Remember: not everything that appears plausible is true! So take another try: you are travelling from A to B; on one way there you drive at 100 mph while returning you only hit 50. What was your average speed on both journeys? 75? Slow down!

See also Hyperbolic Discounting (ch. 51); Decision Fatigue (ch. 53); Exponential Growth (ch. 34); Gambler's Fallacy (ch. 29) and The Problem With Averages (ch. 55) as further resources.

How To Expose Charlatans (Step-by-Step Instructions)

Dear Reader: To my utter surprise, I know you intimately. Here is how I would characterize you: 'You have a strong need for other people to appreciate and admire you; however, you often tend to criticize yourself as well.' Your potential is vastly underused and has yet to be maximized. Although you have some personality flaws, they are typically manageable with some adjustments; however, your sexual adjustment has presented challenges for you. Though outwardly disciplined and controlled, you often feel insecure inside. At times you may question whether you made the appropriate decision or carried out necessary action. Your sense of change and variety makes you uncomfortable, leaving you dissatisfied when the world becomes stagnant or restrictive. As an independent thinker, you don't accept others' statements without adequate proof. Your experience has taught you it is not wise to be too open in revealing yourself to others. Your personality ranges from being outgoing and friendly, at times to introverted and reserved; some of your aspirations might even seem lofty! Security is one of your primary goals in life.'

Do You Recognize Yourself? How Would My Evaluation Go From 1 (Poor) to 5 (Excellent)

Bertram Forer conducted an experiment in 1948 using astrology columns from various magazines to craft an exact passage which could then be given out to his students for reading and assessed, suggesting each person received a personalized assessment. On average, his students gave Forer an accuracy score of 86% which resulted in repeated trials over decades with virtually identical outcomes.

Most likely you rated the text with four or five stars. People tend to recognize many of their own traits when reading universal descriptions - a phenomenon called the Forer effect (or Barnum effect). It explains why pseudosciences like astrology, astrotherapy, handwriting analysis, biorhythm analysis palmistry tarot card readings and seances with dead people work so effectively.

Why does Forer's effect exist? Firstly, Forer made most of his statements in his book on these topics.
Second, these statements apply to everyone: 'Sometimes you seriously doubt your actions.' Nobody would deny that! Thirdly, we tend to accept flattering statements that do not pertain directly to us: 'You are proud of your independent thinking.' Who wouldn't? Fourthly, confirmation bias: we accept information which confirms what we perceive of ourselves while filtering out anything contradictory; what remains is a coherent portrait.

Consultants and analysts can perform similar magic: "This stock has significant growth potential even in a very competitive environment; however, management lacks the impetus to fully realize and implement ideas from its development team. Management are experienced industry professionals; however, signs of bureaucratisation are apparent; savings opportunities exist on its profit and loss statement and we advise the company to focus more closely on emerging economies to secure future market share." Sounds plausible enough?

How can one evaluate an astrologer? For an impartial assessment, select twenty people and assign them each a number. Have the guru characterise each person individually on cards without them discovering who their number was until after receiving all copies. Only when most participants identified 'their' description as accurately described can true talent emerge - I am still waiting!

See also: Feature-Positive Effect (ch. 95); Confirmation Bias (chs. 7-8);

WHY VOLUNTEER WORK IS FOR THE BIRDS

Volunteer's Folly

Jack, a photographer for fashion magazines, spends Monday through Friday traveling between Milan, Paris and New York on assignments from fashion magazines in search of beautiful girls with interesting designs, in pristine lighting conditions. Well known on social circles he brags to his friends that his fee of approximately $500 an hour compares favourably with commercial law rates; "And my shots look much better than any banker!"

Jack leads an enviable lifestyle, yet recently has grown more philosophical. Something has made him question his relationship to fashion: the industry seems selfish to him now and leaves him restless at night, yearning for more fulfilling work that allows him to give back something meaningful back into society - no matter how small.

One day his phone rings. It was Patrick, his former classmate and now President of a local bird club: 'Next Saturday is our annual birdhouse drive - we need volunteers to build birdhouses for endangered species then place them up in the woods after we put up. Please join us! We start meeting at 8 AM; hopefully we'll finish before lunch time'

What should Jack say if he truly cares about creating a better world? Simply, he should decline. Why? Jack earns $500 an hour while carpenters typically make $50. Rather than trying to build quality birdhouses himself (something which would never happen), why not work an extra hour as a photographer and then hire a professional carpenter for six hours to build top quality houses that cannot possibly be done by an amateur himself? His tax return would cover this difference of $200 which could then be donated directly to a bird club? This way his contribution would go much farther.

Jack will likely appear bright and early next Saturday to assemble birdhouses, which economists refer to as the volunteer's folly. Although volunteering is a popular trend; over one-fourth of Americans volunteer their time. Yet economists caution against volunteering for just any cause - volunteering can take away work from tradespeople who might otherwise use those hours productively building birdhouses themselves, instead taking time from them themselves or cobbling together a few birdhouses by hand is likely more efficient - providing him with opportunities that would bring rewards that go far beyond any tangible contribution of this kind that any volunteer activity might provide.
Jack knows his skills can only truly add value when applied directly. For instance, if the bird club were planning a fundraising mail campaign and needed professional photos taken of members for inclusion in its mailings campaign he could either shoot them himself or work

an extra hour to hire another top photographer and donate the remaining funds from hiring another top photographer.

Now we arrive at the contentious topic of altruism: does selflessness exist at all or is it simply a way for us to ease our egos? While volunteerism often serves as an avenue to help their community, personal benefits like skills development and networking opportunities also play a significant role. Suddenly we're no longer acting purely altruistically; many volunteers engage in what might be termed "personal happiness management", with benefits far removed from what was originally intended by volunteering - strictly speaking anyone who benefits or feels any satisfaction from volunteering is not pure altruist

Does Jack make the wrong move by volunteering on Saturday morning? Not necessarily; one group that can buck this tendency are celebrities like Bono, Kate Winslet or Mark Zuckerberg; they provide much-needed publicity when taking part in volunteerism projects involving birdhouse building, beach cleanup or earthquake relief efforts. Therefore Jack must carefully evaluate whether their participation would add anything of value; otherwise the best way for individuals to contribute would likely be with their money rather than hard labor.

See also Deformation Professionalnelle (ch. 92); Omission Bias (ch. 44);

WHY YOU'RE A SERVANT TO YOUR

What do you think about genetically modified wheat? It's an emotional topic and answering too quickly can lead to regrettable decisions; taking an objective approach would require taking into account both its benefits and drawbacks separately. Write down all possible benefits, weigh them according to their importance, and multiply their likelihood by probability - this gives a list of expected values. Now apply this same process when considering potential disadvantages. List all of the disadvantages, estimate their potential damage and multiply that figure by their likelihood. Subtracting out positive sums from negative sums yields the net expected value - if that number is above zero you are pro-GM wheat; otherwise it indicates you oppose it. Undoubtedly you are familiar with this approach to decision theory called expected value, featured widely across decision literature. Yet chances are good that it never crossed your mind to carry out such an evaluation - and certainly none of the professors writing textbooks used this method when selecting their spouses!

No one truly relies on this method for decision-making. First off, our imaginations simply don't stretch far enough; our understanding can only reach so far into what has already come through experience. Imagine an epic storm if you are only 30 years old is difficult, while calculating small probabilities is near impossible due to lack of data about rare events. Thirdly, small probabilities often require less data points and lead to larger errors on exact probabilities - creating an inexorable circle of error. Our brain isn't designed for such calculations either; such calculations require time and effort - not our natural state! In our evolutionary past, those who overthought often met an untimely demise from predators. Today's decision makers rely heavily on mental shortcuts known as heuristics for rapid decision-making processes.

One of the most frequently employed heuristics is the affect heuristic. An affect is an immediate reaction: something you like or dislike; for example, hearing "gunfire" elicits negative associations while hearing "luxury" produces positive ones; this automatic one-dimensional impulse prevents one from taking into account risks and benefits when making decisions.
Instead of treating risks and benefits as independent variables, which they certainly are, an affect heuristic connects them through sensory channels.

Your emotional responses to issues like nuclear power, organic vegetables, private schools and motorbikes determine your assessment of risks and benefits associated with them. If something strikes a chord with you emotionally, its risks appear smaller while its benefits appear greater than they really are; conversely if something you dislike sparks up strong emotions against it; risks and benefits appear to be dependent despite reality showing them otherwise.

Imagine owning a Harley-Davidson. If a study indicates that driving one may be riskier than previously believed, your subconscious mind could respond by rating its benefits differently and giving the experience even greater freedom.

But how is an initial, spontaneous emotion, such as happiness or anger, generated? Researchers at the University of Michigan provided participants with either of three images for less than one hundredth of a second; either smiling faces, angry faces or neutral figures were shown briefly before. Subjects then had to select whether they liked a random Chinese character they'd been shown (without knowing Chinese), with most participants favoring those that immediately preceded a smiling face symbol. Even seemingly insignificant factors can have profound impacts on our emotions. Hirschleifer and Shumway investigated how an otherwise inconsequential factor played a part in market performance of 26 major stock exchanges from 1982-1997 by testing their relationship between sunlight hours per morning and market performance in each exchange. They discovered an intriguing correlation that reads like an old farmer's saying: if the sun shines brightly in the morning, stocks tend to increase throughout the day - not always, but often enough. Who would have thought sunshine could move billions? Morning sunshine seems to have the same positive influence as smiling faces do!

No matter our intentions, our emotions control us. Decisions are often made based on feelings rather than thoughts; against all best intentions we substitute "What do I think about this?" with "How do I feel about this". So smile! Your future depends on it!

See also Association Bias (ch. 48); Loss Aversion (ch. 32), Salience Effect (ch. 83) and Contagion Bias (ch. 54)

Bruce works in the vitamin business. His father started it during an era when supplements weren't yet part of daily lifestyle; doctors would need to prescribe them. When Bruce took over as CEO in the early 90s, demand skyrocketed, prompting him to take out massive loans in order to increase production. Today he stands as one of the most successful individuals in his industry and president of a national association of vitamin manufactures; almost daily since childhood he's taken at least three multivitamins. When interviewed by journalists about it's effectiveness; when asked by journalist if anything they did anything, Bruce replied 'I'm sure of it' - can you believe him?

Here's another challenge for you. Think about any idea or belief you are certain of; perhaps gold will rise over the next five years, God exists, or your dentist is overcharging you - write it all down in one sentence and see if you truly believe yourself!

Aren't you convinced your conviction is more valid than Bruce's? Well, here is why: yours is an internal observation, while Bruce's is external; in other words, you can see into their soul while not into yours.

In Bruce's case, you might think: 'Well, of course it's in his best interests to believe vitamins are beneficial - his wealth and social status depend on their success; all his life he's been taking pills so he won't ever admit that they were waste of time' But for you personally it's different: You have done extensive research inside yourself and come out as completely impartial observers.

But can internal reflection truly be pure and honest? Swedish psychologist Petter Johannson conducted a study where test subjects viewed two portrait photos of random people and chose which face was more appealing; then asked them to describe its most attractive features up close. But with an ingenious ploy - most participants failed to notice he switched images midway - most went on justifying why they preferred an image so thoroughly! His results of his study: introspection isn't reliable: when we conduct soul searches we often make subjective choices - meaning introspection is unreliable: when we conduct internal self-analysis
Contrive findings to achieve desired findings is known as the introspection illusion - this belief that reflection leads to truth or accuracy is more than sophistry, because of our strong-held convictions we tend to experience three reactions when someone doesn't share our viewpoints: Response 1, 2, or 3.

First Response: Assumption of Ignorance. You assume the other party does not possess sufficient knowledge; had they received your knowledge, they may well share your perspective. Political activists tend to think along these lines: they believe enlightenment will persuade others into their camp. Reaction 2: Assumption of Idiocy Response 3: Assumption of Malice. When someone does not grasp an obvious conclusion from available information, and therefore cannot draw the obvious inferences he may appear ignorant and stupid to us all. Bureaucrats especially like using this approach as it protects'stupid' consumers from themselves. Response 1: Lack of Due Process. Your counterpart possesses all of the necessary information - and even comprehends the debate - but is deliberately combative, harboring malicious intentions. Many religious leaders and followers view disbelievers in this same light: If they disagree with them, they must be agents of Satan!

Conclusion: nothing is as convincing as your own beliefs, which is why introspection can provide real self-knowledge. Unfortunately, introspection is often falsified or falsified with too much trust being placed in internal observations too much and too long; secondly, our perception is often higher of ourselves than of others and this creates an illusion of superiority; remedy for both is to become increasingly critical with ourselves - treat internal observations with equal skepticism as claims from third parties; become your toughest critic!

See also Illusion of Control (ch. 17); Self-Serving Bias (ch. 45); Confirmation Bias (chs 7-8) and Not-Invented-Here Syndrome (ch 74) for more on these topics.

Next to my bed are 24 books that are piled high. Though I dip in and out, none can leave my possession. Though I know sporadic reading won't provide me any real insights despite all my hours spent reading, so instead it would make more sense for me to focus on one book at a time; so why am I still juggling all 24 of them at once?

My friend knows a man who is dating three women simultaneously and can see himself starting a family with any one of them, yet he cannot bring himself to choose just one - that would mean passing up on two others permanently; by keeping options open all options remain available, though no real relationships form as a result.

General Xiang Yu, in the third century B.C., sent his army across the Yangtze River to challenge Qin Dynasty. While his troops slept he ordered all ships be set afire; next morning he told them: 'Now you have only one choice: Either fight to win or die.' By eliminating retreat as an option he helped focus their attention solely on battle. Spanish conquistador Cortes used similar motivational tactics during his sixteenth-century conquest of Mexico when after landing on its east coast he sank his own ship as motivation.

Xiang Yu and Cortes stand out as outliers; most people strive to increase our options as much as possible. Psychology professors Dan Ariely and Jiwoong Shin have demonstrated the strength of this instinct through an online game. Players were given 100 points at the beginning, and three doors appeared on screen - red, blue and green doors. Opening each of them cost one point; however, with every room they entered they could earn additional points. Players reacted logically, choosing to remain in one room until its fruition. Ariely and Shin then changed the rules so if doors weren't opened within twelve moves they began shrinking on screen, eventually vanishing altogether; players then raced from door to door in search of potential treasure troves; this unproductive scrambling resulted in them scoring 15% less points than in their prior game. Finally, Ariely and Shin added one final twist: they changed how you scored points by increasing door sizes by 25%! Finally they added another twist: players would still score 10% points this time round! The organisers added another wrinkle with another twist: once more: doors could close within twelve moves when they appeared - forcing players from door-hopping from door-opening as quickly as before! Ariely and Shin then made another change; this time round when doors did not open within twelve moves, doors started shrinking off-screen and eventually vanished off-screen! When Ariely and Shin changed yet again by changing rules: doors had to open within twelve moves or they would disappear off-screen! Players began racing from door-door trying to secure access all potential treasure troves which resulted in 15% less points scored! Ariely and Shin added one final twist: this time round than previous game score 15% less points score 15% less points than before while adding one last twist: the organisers added another twist: once

opened within twelve moves they vanished off screen gradually until eventually vanished before Vanished altogether vanished as doors began shrinking, Ariely changed rules required door was now had been opened within twelve moves otherwise, started shrinking off screen within twelve moves or otherwise immediately vanished making door after 12 moves or their previous scored 15 so quickly so much scraming that before scored 15% less points scoring 15% less points then added another twist by way... The -
Opening doors now cost three points and the same anxiety set in: players wasted away their points trying to keep all doors open. Even after learning how many points were hidden in each room, there was no change; forgoing options was too great an expense for them.

Why do we act irrationally? Because its consequences are often not clear-cut. On financial markets, for instance, this is evident: any option on a security always costs something; there is no such thing as a free option; yet in other realms options often appear free; though in truth these too come at a cost; each decision requires mental energy and takes away precious time for thinking and living; CEOs who explore every possible expansion option often select none in the end; companies which attempt to serve all customer segments often fail; salespeople who pursue leads often end up closing no deals despite all efforts.

People today tend to be fixated on having numerous projects going at once and being open to every opportunity that presents itself; but this approach can quickly derail success. Instead, we must learn when and why to close doors; business strategies serve mainly as statements on which activities not to engage in. Use a similar approach as businesses: list what not to pursue in life and make calculated decisions not to pursue certain possibilities; when an option arises, test it against your not-to-pursue list before taking further steps. Not only will a list help keep you out of trouble, but it will also save time spent making decisions. With your list in hand, instead of making decisions every time a new door opens up - many doors don't make sense even when their handles seem easy enough - all you have to do is refer back to it when making choices.

See Also: Sunk Cost Fallacy (Ch. 5);

WARNING ABOUT NEOMANIA

In fifty years time, what will our world look like and which items will surround us daily? It's easy to get caught up in Neomania; let's put aside any "brand new".

People pondering this question fifty years ago had fantastical ideas of what 'the future' would look like: highways in the skies, cities resembling glass worlds and bullet trains zooming along between skyscrapers. We would live in plastic capsules underwater cities vacationing on the moon taking pills instead of having biological children conceived through conception; instead choose children from catalogues to be our children; robots would become best friends instead of people as companions while death had long since been eradicated - the picture they imagined was not far away!

But wait a second: take a close look around you: you are sitting in a chair created in ancient Egypt; wearing pants developed about 5,000 years ago by Germanic tribes around 750 B.C; the leather shoes on your feet originated during the last ice age; your bookshelves are composed of wood - one of the oldest building materials known to man; at dinnertime you use your fork as it was used by Romans: to shovel chunks of dead animals and plants into your mouths at dinner time - nothing has changed - nothing has changed either;

Are we wondering what our world will look like in fifty years? Nassim Taleb offers us some guidance in his book Antifragile; take into account that most technologies that have existed over the past half-century will continue to serve humanity for another half-century - while recent technology will become outdated more quickly than expected. Why? Think of inventions as species: anything that has withstood centuries of evolution will likely keep going strong into the future, too. Old technology is proven; its inherent logic cannot always be fully comprehended. You should take this into consideration the next time you attend a strategy meeting, since something that has persisted over centuries must have some value. Fifty years into the future will likely resemble today, although you may see new flashy gadgets or inventions emerge that might spark interest at first. Yet they often come and go quickly.

When considering our futures, we often put too much emphasis on technological innovations and "killer apps", while underestimating their role.
Taleb has observed this tendency throughout history. In the 1960s, space travel was all the rage, leading many students to imagine themselves taking school trips to Mars. Later on in the decade plastic houses became fashionable so we thought about how we'd decorate our see-through dwellings with plastic furniture. He attributes this tendency back to "neomania", the fascination for all things new and shiny.

At first I felt sympathy for early adopters - those people who cannot live without having access to the latest iPhone. At that time I thought they were ahead of their time; now, however, I view them as irrational individuals suffering from neomania - they seem less concerned with whether a product provides tangible benefits but more concerned with novelty than actual utility.

Don't take drastic measures when forecasting the future. Stanley Kubrick's 1968 classic film 2001: A Space Odyssey serves as an illustration. Set at the turn of the millennium, this visionary piece predicted that America would host a thousand-strong moon colony, serviced by PanAm commuter flights - something no-one saw coming. I suggest this rule of thumb instead: whatever has survived for X years will continue doing so for another X years - Nassim Taleb believes history's "bullshit filter" can separate gimmicks from game-changers so I am willing to make that bet with him!

See Also Hedonic Treadmill (ch. 46) as an Example of Why Propaganda Works.
World War II saw every nation create propaganda movies. These were used to stir nationalist feelings among civilians and soldiers alike and encourage sacrifice for their nation. After spending an exorbitant amount on propaganda films alone, the U.S. war department conducted studies into whether this expenditure had any return. Studies were done involving regular soldiers; their response did not show an increase in enthusiasm for war at all!

Did the soldiers view these movies as poorly made? Hardly. Rather, soldiers knew these movies as propaganda that made it all but impossible for any message presented in these films to have any weight with audiences; even if a movie made an argument or stirred audiences sufficiently to merit consideration or appreciation for its message; its content would simply be seen as hollow and disregarded outright.

Nine weeks later, something unexpected transpired: psychologists conducted another evaluation of soldiers' attitudes regarding war; the result: those who had watched the movie expressed much more support than those who hadn't. Evidentially, propaganda did work!

Scientists were bemused, knowing that an argument's persuasive power decreases over time, like radioactive material. You've probably experienced this yourself: read an article on gene therapy's benefits, become enthusiastic at first but quickly lose interest after some weeks; finally only remnants of enthusiasm remain.

Amazingly, propaganda often works the other way: once it strikes a chord with people, its impact only grows over time. Why? Psychologist Carl Hovland led an experiment for the war department and coined this phenomenon "Sleeper Effect." Currently, our best explanation for it is that our memories forget the source faster than it forgets what the argument itself

(e.g. Department of Propaganda) said while remembering the message itself (i.e. War is necessary and noble).
Therefore, information gained from untrustworthy sources gradually gains trust over time as discrediting forces dissipate faster than their message does.

U.S. elections increasingly feature negative political ads in which candidates attempt to disparage each other's records or reputations through deceptively simple means - in this instance, political ads must comply with US electioneering law by disclosing their sponsors at the end of every ad, yet numerous studies show that sleeper effects still play out among undecided voters as the messenger fades while their statements remain imprinted upon memory - this allows candidates to launch the most damaging accusations possible against rival candidates without fear of reprisals or consequences being issued against either side if the end result would be less negative than expected by law - this makes electioneering ads much harder a process than it ought to be used against rival campaigns by opponents from both sides in campaigns in terms of voter turnout or turnout numbers than otherwise possible in campaign seasons prior.

I have often found it puzzling how advertising can work at all. Any logical person should easily recognize ads for what they are and disqualify or categorise them appropriately; yet even you as a discerning and intelligent reader won't always succeed at doing this successfully; you may forget where certain information came from after several weeks - be it an informative article or tacky advertorial!

How can you counter the sleeper effect? First, be wary of any unsolicited advice even if it seems well intended - doing this protects yourself against manipulation to some degree. Second, avoid sources with ads as much as possible (we're lucky books remain ad-free!). Thirdly, identify and remember who the source of each argument you encounter was. Try to understand their reasoning as much as possible as well as who benefits from what. Although this process might slow down decision making processes somewhat but will also refine them over time.

See also Framing (ch. 42); Primacy and Recency Effects (ch. 73); News Illusion (ch. 99).

Why Is Racing Never Just Two Horse Race?

Alternative Blindness

Imagine this: you're flipping through a brochure touting the benefits of an MBA degree offered at your local university. Your gaze flits over photographs of its ivy-covered campus and ultramodern sports facilities; alongside images of smiling students from diverse ethnic backgrounds with an emphasis on young women, Chinese, and Indian go-getters. Finally you reach an overview that illustrates its financial worth: its $100,000 fee can easily be offset by graduates generating extra earnings before retiring: roughly $400,000 after taxes! No brainer.

Wrong. Such an argument conceals not one, but four fallacies. First is "swimmer's body illusion", in that MBA programmes tend to attract career-minded individuals who will likely command above-average salaries without additional qualifications such as an MBA qualification. The second myth: an MBA takes two years and during that time you can expect a loss of earnings of $100,000; therefore the true cost of an MBA would likely exceed $100,000 when factoring in potential returns from investing. Thirdly, making estimates more than thirty years out is foolish - who knows what will happen over that timeframe? Finally, other options exist; don't feel bound by 'do an MBA or don't do an MBA' alone. Perhaps there is another programme available that costs significantly less and also offers career advancement benefits. I find the fourth misconception particularly fascinating; let's call it alternative blindness: when we fail to compare an existing offer with its next-best alternative offer.

Here's an example from finance: imagine you have some money saved up in a savings account and ask an investment broker for advice, who recommends purchasing a bond that pays 5% interest instead of just the 1% that savings accounts give back. Do we think buying the bond makes sense? No one knows. Considering only these two choices would not provide an accurate assessment; to truly assess all possible investment choices then select the optimal one (this is how top investor Warren Buffet does it).
Buffett measures each transaction against the second-best deal that's available at any given moment - even if that means doing more of what we already are doing.'

Contrary to Warren Buffett, politicians often fall prey to alternative blindness. Consider your city planning on building a sports arena on an empty plot of land; supporters might argue it will benefit residents more emotionally and financially than an empty lot - however this comparison is flawed: instead they should evaluate all ideas which become impossible due to its construction such as schools, performing arts centres, hospitals or incinerators; alternatively they could sell the land off and invest the proceeds or reduce city debt with this alternative solution.

Are You Overlooking Alternative Solutions? Imagine Your Doctor Discovers A Tumor In Five Years And Proposes A Complicated Operation That If Successful Would Remove it Completely But However The Risk Is Considered High With an overall Survival Rate of Just 50% How do you decide? Consider your options carefully: certain death in five years or a 50% chance of dying next week; alternative blindness! Perhaps there is a variant of an invasive surgery procedure available at another hospital in town that doesn't currently offer it at your institution. Surgery to slow tumor growth could only temporarily alleviate symptoms; however, this invasive surgery provides more time and peace of mind than its alternatives; who knows, maybe during those ten years more advanced therapies for eliminating tumours will emerge?

Bottom line: If you're having difficulty making decisions, remember that there are more than two options - such as no surgery and high risk surgery - available to you. Don't feel trapped between an absolute choice and its possible alternatives; be open-minded!

See Paradox of Choice (ch. 21); Swimmer's Body Illusion (ch. 2) for further reading on these subjects.

WHY WE AIM AT YOUNG GUNNS

SOCIAL COMPARISON BIAS

After my book reached #1 on the bestseller list, my publisher asked for my help in providing an endorsement for another title by an acquaintance on its way into the top ten list; they believed a testimonial from me would give it that extra push into being included on that list.

Always amazed that these testimonials work at all, given how we all know only positive comments make it onto book jackets (this book included). A rational reader must put aside praise or at least consider it alongside any potential criticism which is always present, even if in different forms. While I have written many testimonials for other books, none were for rival titles. As I considered my options, I realized social comparison bias had taken effect - that tendency to avoid helping those who could soon overshadow you and look foolish in the long run.

Book testimonials can serve as a harmless example of social comparison bias; however, academia has taken this to an altogether more dangerous level. Every scientist aspires to publish as many articles in prestigious scientific journals, earning himself or herself the right to assess submissions from fellow scientists submitting work for publication. Over time, editors ask you to assess other scientists' submissions - often only two or three experts decide which articles make the cut in any given field; with this knowledge in mind, what would happen when an upstart researcher submits an earthshaking paper that threatens to overthrow established experts? They would likely become particularly rigorous when evaluating it - this is social comparison bias at work!

Psychologer Stephen Garcia and his fellow researchers describe an example in which a Nobel laureate barred one of his promising young colleagues from applying to work at "his" university, although this might appear prudent initially; over time it becomes counterproductive when said young colleague joins another research group - potentially precluding any further contact between the old professor and him or her and this young prodigy.
Garcia suggests that social comparison bias may be one factor preventing institutions from maintaining their status as world-class research groups over an extended period. Few research groups manage to remain at the top for many years running.

Social comparison bias is another significant issue with start-up companies. Guy Kawasaki served as Apple's 'chief evangelist' for four years and today advises entrepreneurs as a venture capitalist and advisor. According to Kawasaki: 'A-players hire people even better than themselves. As Steve [Jobs] stated, B-players recruit C-players so they can feel superior to them and C-players recruit D-players; when hiring B-players expect what he termed "the bozo explosion" to take place within your organization; hiring B-players eventually results in hiring Z-players instead of B-players. Recommendation: Hire people who are better than yourself or else you will soon lead a team of underdogs. The so-called Duning-Kruger effect applies here; Z-players with incompetence often have the gift of overlooking its extent, believing they possess more intelligence than is actually there; such people create an illusionary superiority which leads them into making even more mistakes which in turn erode the talent pool over time.

Isaac Newton was 25-years old at the time and when his school closed due to an outbreak of plague in 1666-7, Isaac Barrow offered to come along and see his research, which Barrow immediately left as professor to join as one of Newton's students - it was truly noble of him! What an ethical example it set. And when was the last time you heard about a professor stepping aside in favor of another candidate or CEO giving their position away due to realising one of their employees could do better job?

Conclusion: In conclusion, do you foster individuals more talented than yourself? While it might threaten your standing initially, in the long run it will only benefit. Others will overtake you at some stage anyway; until that time arrives it would be wise to get on their good sides and learn from them - which was my motivation in writing the testimonial at the end. For further reading see: Envy (ch. 86); Contrast Effect (ch. 10).

PRIMACY AND RECENCY EFFECTS

Let me introduce two men, Alan and Ben. Immediately decide who you prefer without overthinking it too long: Alan is smart, hard-working, impulsive, critical, stubborn and jealous while Ben's qualities include these characteristics but with a twist: Ben can also be jealous, stubborn, critical impulsive hard working smart as well. Most people choose Alan even though both descriptions sound similar. Your brain tends to pay more attention to adjectives listed first thus creating two distinct personalities - Alan is hard-working while Ben displays jealousy and stubborn traits - something known as primacy effect.

Without the primacy effect, people would forgoing lavish entrance halls at their headquarters; your attorney would feel just as content to appear wearing worn-out sneakers rather than designer Oxfords for your meetings.

The primacy effect often causes practical errors. Nobel laureate Daniel Kahneman discusses how, at the start of his professorship, he graded examination papers in order: student 1 followed by student 2, then all subsequent questions flawlessly answered were given higher scores; this meant students who answered perfectly would become favorites of Kahneman and this would ultimately have an effect on how he graded other parts of their exams. To counteract this effect, Kahneman started to grade individual questions in batches - all answers to question 1 being graded, then all answers to question 2 etc - thus counteracting this effect and neutralising it altogether.

Unfortunately, this trick may not always work in practice; for instance when hiring new employees you risk hiring the person who makes a good first impression first. To maximize efficiency when answering similar questions one by one from all candidates in line.

Imagine yourself as part of a company board. A discussion topic arises on which you haven't made up your mind yet, and one or more participants present express an opinion that may influence how you evaluate it overall. Don't hesitate to voice it before others do - that way all can learn.
By doing this, you will gain more influence with your colleagues and bring them over to your side. If chairing a committee, make sure to gather opinions in random order so no one has an unfair edge over another member.

Primacy effect may not always be at fault; recency effect often plays an equally influential role. Information stored more recently tends to stick better in our memory - this happens because our short-term memory files only contain limited space; as soon as something new comes along, an older piece must make way.

When does primacy trump recency effect, and vice versa? When faced with making immediate decisions based on multiple impressions (characteristics, exam answers etc), primacy effects weigh heavier. But if these impressions were formed over a longer time frame - for instance if you listened to a speech recently then recency effect is more prominent; you will remember more clearly its final points/punchlines rather than initial ones.

Conclusion: Initial and last impressions dominate, meaning the content between has only minimal bearing. Try to avoid making decisions based solely on initial impressions; these will undoubtedly deceive you in some form or another. Assess all aspects fairly and impartially - though this may be easier said than done - such as conducting interviews by taking note of scores every five minutes and then averaging them out afterwards to make sure all aspects count equally such as hello and goodbye scores.

See also Illusion of Attention (ch. 88); Sleeper Effect (ch. 70); Salience Effect (ch. 83)

WHY HOME-MADE IS BEST

Not-Invented-Here Syndrome

My cooking abilities are rather basic, and my wife knows it. Every so often though, I manage to create something edible. Recently, when purchasing some sole, I created an unusual sauce made up of white wine, pureed pistachio nuts, honey, grated orange peel and balsamic vinegar - and when she tasted it she began scraping off what she saw as too bold of an experiment; but I thought it tasted wonderful and explained its details but no change could be seen on her expression.

Two weeks later, my wife prepared sole for dinner again, this time cooking it herself. She prepared two sauces: her tried-and-true beurre blanc sauce as well as an unusual recipe from a top French chef that tasted terrible; later revealed as Swiss instead! Clearly she caught me off guard; I had succumbed to Not-Invented-Here Syndrome (NIH syndrome), wherein any creation you create yourself becomes superior in comparison with anything that comes after.

NIH Syndrome causes people to fall in love with their own ideas. This applies not only to fish sauce recipes, but all forms of solutions, business ideas and inventions developed internally; companies often rate such concepts as more significant than any from external sources; however this may not necessarily be accurate in reality. Recently I met with the CEO of a software provider for health insurance firms. He explained how difficult it was for his firm - even though it led the market in terms of service, security, and functionality - to sell their software products directly to potential customers. Many insurers believe their own in-house solutions provide the optimal solutions, yet another CEO told me how difficult it was to convince his staff at headquarters to accept solutions proposed from far-flung subsidiaries.

When people collaborate to solve problems and evaluate these ideas themselves, the NIH syndrome will unavoidably manifest itself and take its course. Thus it inevitably has an impactful result which results in its impactful manifestation. This makes the condition all the more significant.

Splitting teams into two groups makes sense: one will generate ideas while the other rates them, with ideas generated by one team being evaluated by another, then reversed - this way both groups get equal time at creating ideas and rating concepts from another. We tend to evaluate our own business ideas more positively than those proposed by others - an attribute essential for entrepreneurial success yet often leading to disappointing returns in start-up businesses.

Psychologe Dan Ariely used his blog at The New York Times to quantify NIH Syndrome. Ariely requested readers provide solutions to six problems, such as "How can cities reduce water consumption without being limited by law?," making suggestions and evaluating feasibility; further specifying time and money investments into each idea proposed; finally using only fifty words so all responses provided matched exactly. Regardless, most readers rated their responses more important and applicable than their fellow contributors even when the submissions were practically identical.

On a societal level, the NIH syndrome can have disastrous results. We often dismiss intelligent ideas from other cultures simply because we cannot appreciate their proven merits. Switzerland, where each state or canton (pronounced cantonessalee in French) possesses certain powers, was home to an unusual case of National Involvement in Health (NIH) when one small canton refused to approve women's suffrage despite an outraged federal court ruling in 1990 that effectively changed it - another glaring example of National Intervention in Health. Consider also the modern traffic roundabout designed by British transport engineers during the 1960s and implemented throughout Britain. It boasts stringent yield requirements. After several decades of oblivion and resistance, traffic decongestion measures such as roundabouts eventually spread throughout both North America and continental Europe. France alone now boasts over 30,00 roundabouts that many Frenchpeople mistakenly attribute to its creator, who designed the Place de l'Etoile.

Conclusion: we tend to get carried away with our own ideas, making us increasingly drunk with their power. To stay sober and evaluate their quality objectively in hindsight - which of your ideas from the last ten years were truly outstanding? Exactly.

See also Introspection Illusion (ch. 67); Endowment Effect (ch. 23); Self-Serving Bias (ch. 45); False Consensus Effect (ch. 77)

"All swans are white." For centuries, this statement held true. Every snowy specimen was evidence of this claim; any other color? Unthinkable. That was until 1697, when Willem de Vlamingh first encountered a black swan on an expedition to Australia; since then black swans have come to symbolize improbabilities in life.

One day in 1987 was such a day - Nassim Taleb famously described this event in his book by giving no warning of its outcome! A Black Swan event.

Black Swan events are unimaginable events that dramatically transform life, career and society - from meteorites that strike you down to Sutter's discovery of gold in California or Sutter's death; from Sutter's discovery to Sputnik and Internet browser development; or another encounter which completely upturns lives - each are potential Black Swans that could have positive or negative ramifications - these all qualify as Black Swans.

Donald Rumsfeld was once famous for articulating a powerful philosophical thought at a press conference: there are things we know for certain ('known facts'), some things that remain unknown (known unknowns), and those things which remain hidden or mysterious to us ('unknown unknowns').

Are we currently exploring the size and scope of the universe, the presence of nuclear weapons in Iran, or whether or not the Internet makes us smarter or dumber? These questions represent 'known unknowns', with which with enough effort we may one day hope to provide answers; unlike unknown unknowns such as Facebook mania which no one anticipated at its inception ten years ago: it was truly unexpected and unpredictable.

Why are Black Swans important? Although it may sound strange, Black Swans have been increasingly occurring over time and tend to become increasingly consequential. While we can plan for our futures with certainty, unexpected events such as Black Swans can often leave us scrambling in response.
Feedback loops and nonlinear influences often subvert our best intentions, leading to unexpected outcomes. One reason is our brains' inherent ability to hunt and gather. In Stone Age times, hunters rarely encountered anything truly extraordinary - our deer chased were often slower or faster, fattier or thinner. Everything tended towards a steady mean.

Today is different; one breakthrough can multiply your income by an order of magnitude - just ask Larry Page, Usain Bolt, George Soros, J.K. Rowling or Bono for examples. Before now such fortunes were unimaginable - only recently have such feats been possible and lead to our modern-day fear of extreme scenarios. Since probabilities cannot fall below zero and human thoughts often exhibit errors, you should assume everything has an above-zero probability.

What can be done? Place yourself in situations that could allow for you to catch a ride.

Create the possibility for yourself of being lucky enough to experience a positive Black Swan event (although that is extremely unlikely). Consider becoming an artist, inventor or entrepreneur with a scalable product. Selling your time as an employee, dentist or journalist won't do - though even if forced into continuing this path avoid environments which could allow negative Black Swan events to arise.
Stay out of debt, invest your savings as conservatively as possible, and accept living on a modest standard of living regardless of whether or not your big breakthrough occurs.

Notes on Ambiguity Aversion (ch. 80); Forecast Illusion (ch. 40); Alternative Paths (ch. 39) and Expectations (ch. 62) from this book.

Writing books about clear thinking brings many rewards: business leaders and investors are happy to pay me to give talks on it for good money, though that seems odd since books are much cheaper. At one medical conference I gave a talk on base rate neglect using an analogy from medicine: in particular when discussing stabbing chest pain among 40 year-old patients it may indicate heart disease or simply stress - stress being much more likely (with a higher base rate), so it would be prudent to test first for this possibility before testing for heart conditions or stress - something all doctors understood intuitively when I used an economics example; however most faltered when trying to understand this idea in detail compared with analogies from medicine or medicine in general compared with when using an economics example from medicine this analogy most faltered miserably when explaining this aspect of base rate neglect: when using an economics example most faltered when speaking about base rate neglect (base-rate neglect is easier).

As with investors, when speaking in front of an audience I experience similar phenomena: when using examples from finance or economics to illustrate fallacies quickly catch on; but if I use examples from biology they seem lost - showing how insights do not pass easily between fields - an effect known as domain dependence.

Harry Markowitz won the 1990 Nobel Prize in Economics for his theory of "Portfolio Selection". This process determines the optimal composition of a portfolio, taking into account both risk and return considerations. When applied to Markowitz's own savings - how to allot them among stocks and bonds - he simply chose 50/50 distribution. A Nobel Prize recipient couldn't apply his methodological process effectively in his personal affairs; an obvious case of domain dependence; therefore failing to transfer knowledge from academia into daily life.

My friend is an adrenaline enthusiast. He enjoys scaling overhanging cliffs with his bare hands and jumping off mountains in a wingsuit, among other adventurous pursuits. Last week he told me why starting a business can be risky; bankruptcy cannot always be excluded as an option. When we discussed his point, I responded 'Personally, I'd rather be bankrupt than dead!' He didn't appreciate my reasoning!

As an author, I understand the difficulty in transitioning from one area of expertise to another. Plotting novels and creating characters comes easily to me; blank pages don't scare me! On the other hand, dealing with empty boxes and screens is something quite different altogether.
Interior decor can be daunting; I can spend hours staring into space without an idea in mind.

Businesses often rely on domain dependency. A software company might hire an effective consumer-goods salesperson and find that transitioning his talents from consumer products to services sales proves exceedingly challenging. A presenter who excels when speaking to small groups might falter once his audience surpasses 100 people; or an adept marketer may suddenly lack any strategic creativity as he transitions from CEO role.

Markowitz provides us with an example that highlights how difficult the transition from professional to private life can be. I know of CEOs who excel as leaders at work yet seem like empty shells when it comes time for intimate relations outside their office walls. As is often the case, doctors are the worst offending profession when it comes to smoking cigarettes and using tobacco products. Police officers tend to be twice as violent in the home compared to civilians while literary critics receive poor reviews for their books. Couples therapists tend to have more tenuous marriages than their clients; according to mathematics professor Barry Mazur. "Several years ago I was trying to decide whether or not I should move from Stanford to Harvard." After boring my friends with endless discussion, one suggested I put together a list of costs and benefits, along with my expected utility to roughly calculate. Without thinking, my response was: 'Come on Sandy, this is serious.'" Without thinking through my response properly, my response was:

Transferring knowledge from one area to the next can be challenging, particularly between academic and real life settings - and particularly between academia and real life settings such as academia versus real life scenarios. Unfortunately, this applies even for this book's knowledge: you may struggle to apply it in daily life; even for me as its writer that transition proved to be tough! Book smarts don't easily translate to street smarts.

See also Deformation Professionale (ch. 92); Chauffeur Knowledge (ch. 16) and Twaddle Tendency (ch. 57)

THE MYTH OF LIKE-MINDEDNESS

Which music do you prefer: 60s or 80s music? How would the general public respond? People tend to project their preferences onto others; those who love the 1960s might assume most others do too; similarly, 1980s enthusiasts might assume most other people share their taste in music as well. We may often overestimate unanimity among people around us and assume everyone agrees with our thoughts and beliefs--this phenomenon is known as the False-Consensus Effect.

Stanford psychologist Lee Ross first explored this in 1977 by creating a sandwich board emblazoned with the slogan 'Eat at Joe's' and asking randomly selected students to wear it around campus for thirty minutes, estimating how many other students would volunteer themselves for it; those willing to wear the sign assumed that most other people (62%) would agree, while those politely declining believed most (67%) would find the idea too stupid; both groups of students imagined themselves to be part of the popular majority.

The false-consensus effect can be observed among interest groups and political factions that consistently overestimate their causes' popularity, such as global warming. No matter how vital you find this issue to be, most likely you believe most other people share your viewpoint on it. Politicians likewise tend to overestimate their popularity due to an inherent optimism bias which cannot help but make them believe their election prospects are greater than they really are.

Artists fare even worse: when embarking on new projects, artists expect more success than ever before. My personal example was my novel Massimo Marini being an unmitigated success; after all, it had done well compared with its predecessors (though these had also received positive reviews), which seemed equally good in my estimation. Unfortunately for me though, public opinion disagreed and proved me wrong: this phenomenon known as false-consensus effect.

And this applies equally in business: just because an R&D department believes its product will appeal to consumers doesn't mean consumers do too. Companies led by tech professionals tend to make decisions with this bias in mind.
Inventors tend to become entranced by their products' advanced features and incorrectly assume these will captivate customers as well.

The false-consensus effect is fascinating for another reason. When people don't share our opinions, we quickly label them as abnormal or suspicious. Ross' experiment corroborated this; students wearing sandwich boards saw those who did not agree as arrogant or self-centered while those in another camp viewed them as attention seekers or signs-wearers as idiots and noise makers.

Perhaps you recall the fallacy of social proof - the idea that an idea becomes better as more people subscribe to it - which suggests a false consensus effect similar to that seen during false-consensus elections. No. Social proof is an evolutionary survival strategy. Following the crowd has saved our skin more often over the last 100,000 years than going it alone. Although no outside influences are involved in creating false-consensus effects, they still serve a social function; hence evolution did not eliminate them. Our brains were not created to recognize truth; their purpose is instead to produce offspring as many times as possible. Whoever was perceived as courageous and convincing (via the false-consensus effect) left an impressive first impression, attracted more resources, and increased their chances of passing their genes on to future generations. Doubters were seen as less appealing.

Conclusion: Acknowledging that your worldview does not resonate with public sentiment is only half the battle - don't assume those with different ideas are idiots before dismissing them completely and distrusting them, first take a hard, objective look at your assumptions and try challenging yourself before reacting negatively towards those with different viewpoints.

See also Social Proof (Ch. 4) and Not-Invented-Here Syndrome (Ch. 75) for further discussion of these concepts.

Ambiguity Aversion

Two boxes. Box A contains 100 balls: 50 red and 50 black. In Box B, no matter which one is chosen without looking, 100 of the same size but no knowledge as to which ones will be red or black balls if any are pulled from there by accident - should a red ball come out, you win $100! Which box would you pick: A or B? Most people tend to select A as the option.

Play again using exactly the same boxes, and try drawing out one black ball this time for $100! Which box would you select this time around? Most likely it would be A; however, in logic terms B would contain less red balls (and thus more black balls), thus justifying your choice this time around.

Error is common; don't fret: this phenomenon is known as the Ellsberg Paradox and named after Daniel Ellsberg, a former Harvard psychologist (he later leaked top-secret Pentagon Papers to press which eventually caused President Nixon to resign). The Ellsberg Paradox provides empirical proof that we tend to favor familiar probabilities over unknown ones (box A over box B).

So we come back to risk and uncertainty (or ambiguity) and their differences. Risk means that probabilities are known; uncertainly is when probabilities remain unknown; by taking risk into consideration you can decide whether or not taking a gamble makes sense. Uncertainty makes making decisions even harder, and often leads to catastrophic outcomes. Risk and uncertainty are easily confused - often leading to dire repercussions for anyone attempting to make calculations with one versus the other. Statistics is an ancient 300-year-old science that examines risk. Numerous professors study its concepts; however, no textbook exists on uncertainty; so we try to fit uncertainty into risk categories without it making much sense. Below are two examples where this theory works and one where it doesn't: one from medicine (where it works well) and one from economics (where it does not).

Humans make up billions on earth. Our bodies don't vary significantly, reaching similar heights and ages (nobody will ever become 100 feet tall).
One may live for 10,000 years (or only milliseconds!). Most humans possess two eyes, four heart valves and 32 teeth; this means we would appear similar to mice from another species' perspective. Due to this, when dealing with diseases that share similar traits such as cancer, it makes sense to say, for instance: 'There is a 30% risk you will die of cancer.' On the other hand, asserting that "there is a 30% chance the euro will collapse within five years" would not make sense at all. Why? The economy resides in an environment of unpredictability. No

currency history allows us to derive probabilities with any certainty; and the difference between risk and uncertainty also illustrates why life insurance and credit default swaps differ significantly. Credit default swaps (CDSs) are insurance policies against specific defaults of companies' inability to pay, much like life insurance covers risks in an easily calculable form; CDSs introduce uncertainty into our lives which contributed to 2008 financial turmoil. When phrases like 'the risk of hyperinflation is x percent' or 'our equity position is at risk y percent' are heard, take note: they should raise red flags.

To avoid hasty judgements, you must learn to accept ambiguity. Unfortunately, this can be a challenging and insurmountable task which you cannot influence directly. Your amygdala plays an essential role here - this nut-sized area at the center of the brain responsible for memory processing and emotions plays a pivotal role here too: its shape determines your ability or lack thereof in dealing with uncertainty; your political leanings reflect this dynamic as your tolerance of uncertainty differs depending on its construction; in many ways this ties into how often your vote leans towards conservatism - evidenced in part due to biological causes behind their political leanings!

Whoever wishes to think clearly must understand the distinction between risk and uncertainty. Only in certain instances can we rely on clear probabilities - casinos, coin tosses or probability textbooks can provide such assurance - often we are left with troubling ambiguities which require patience in handling. Learn to accept it all as part of life!

See also: Black Swan (ch. 75); Neglect of Probability (ch. 26); Base Rate Neglect (ch. 28); Availability Bias (ch. 11) and Alternative Paths (ch. 39) for further considerations. (82-91).

WHY DO YOU CONTINUE WITH THE STATUS QUO

At a restaurant recently, I perused their wine list in desperation: Irouleguy? Harslevelu? Susumaniello? Although not an expert, it was obvious that their sommelier was trying to impress us with his worldly selections. Finally on page eight was redemption in form of "Our French House Wine: Reserve du Patron, Bourgogne $52". Immediately ordering one thought "Surely this can't be any worse...".

Since I purchased an iPhone several years ago, it has allowed me to customize everything - data usage, app synchronisation, encryption settings and camera shutter sound volume levels among them - to my exact specifications. But you might guess correctly: none have yet been configured!

At my core, I'm not technically challenged; rather I'm simply another victim of the "default effect." When something feels comfortable and inviting to us, we tend to stick with its default setting - like house wine and factory cellphone settings in which we usually settle happily. Just like myself, many other people prefer standard options over individual choices - for instance when buying new cars many buyers tend to select the default color regardless of its availability in other models; many buyers select it regardless. Many opt for default over anything else!

In their book Nudge, economist Richard Thaler and law professor Cass Sunstein illustrate how governments can effectively guide its citizens without violating constitutionally protected freedom. Authorities only need to offer some options - always including an "out" for those unable to decide between them - in order for people to make an informed decision about car-insurance policies for themselves and their neighbors. New Jersey and Pennsylvania demonstrated this with two car-insurance policies provided to their inhabitants. New Jersey advertised this policy as its standard option and most people were happy to accept its lower cost and waiver of certain compensation rights should an accident take place. Pennsylvania drivers seemed more inclined towards choosing the second, more costly option as their standard choice, and quickly made this their top seller. This result was quite remarkable given that both states' drivers are generally similar.
Coverage may differ, depending on what an individual prefers and their desired budget.

Consider this experiment: there is an acute shortage of organ donors, yet only 40% opt for organ donation. Eric Johnson and Dan Goldstein conducted a poll asking people whether, upon death, they wanted actively opt out. By making organ donation the default option rather than opt-in/opt-out defaulting, take-up increased dramatically from 40% to over 80%! This showed the huge difference between an opt-in default vs an opt-out default approach.

When no standard option is specified, we tend to make do with whatever default setting exists and extend and validate its current state. Human nature prefers what they know; given a choice between trying something new or sticking with what we already know, many tend to favor sticking with what's familiar despite knowing any change would benefit them; my bank charges me $60 annually to mail account statements out; downloading them instead would save this expense, yet somehow this service still irks me; maybe because it feels safe enough?

So where does status-quo bias stem from? Loss aversion plays an integral part in this phenomenon. Losses affect us twice as strongly as gains do and that makes tasks such as contract renegotiations extremely challenging - every concession you give out weighs twice as heavily than anything you receive back, creating net losses through such exchanges.

Both the default effect and status-quo bias demonstrate our strong proclivity for sticking with how things are, even if this puts us at a disadvantage. By altering human behavior through setting default settings differently, you can influence human decisions more successfully.

"Maybe our lives follow a grand, hidden default concept," I suggested to a dinner companion, hoping to provoke him into deep philosophical discussion. Instead, after sampling Reserve du Patron wine he stated simply,'maybe it just needs time."
See also Decision Fatigue (ch. 53); Paradox of Choice (ch. 21); Loss Aversion (ch. 32).

WHY "LAST CHANCE' MAKE US PANIC

Fear of Regret | | Paul owns shares in company A, but during the year was considering selling them and purchasing shares from company B instead - ultimately opting not to do so and realizing today he would have netted an extra $1,200 had he done so instead. Meanwhile George owned shares from company B but sold them in order to purchase A shares instead; today both men realize they could have made out better sticking with B instead and gained an extra $1200 profit had they stuck it out longer; who feels more regret? Paul or George?

Regret is the feeling of making the wrong decision, wishing someone would give us another chance. When asked who would feel worse after making a poor choice, only 8% chose Paul while 92% selected George despite both situations being identical: both Paul and George made poor stock choices that left them out of pocket by an equal amount; Paul already owned shares in A while George had to purchase them himself, Paul being passive while George acting actively - it appears those who do not follow mainstream logic experience more regret.

Not always is acting the source of regret; sometimes inaction can create more of an emotional impact than doing something about it. Take, for example, a publishing house which stands alone in refusing to publish trendy e-books; its owner asserts books should remain printed on paper as tradition dictates. Shortly afterwards, nine publishers with plans for launching e-book strategies had failed; this left only conventional paper publishers left standing before going bankrupt - including one which tried but ultimately gave up and went the way of the conventional publisher with traditional publishing houses being the final victim; ultimately, who felt most about this series of decisions made? And who won over most support? Right: the conventional paper-only publisher with its traditional stance against publishing trendy e-grumbler!

Consider Daniel Kahneman's book Thinking, Fast and Slow as an example: After every plane crash, we hear of an individual who intended to fly a day earlier or later but for whatever reason changed their booking at the last minute - creating an exception who garners our sympathy more than those 'normal' passengers on board the ill-fated flight from its outset.

Fear of regret can make us act irrationally; to avoid its unwelcome grip on us, we often act conservatively so as not to deviate too far from what others expect of us. No one is immune; even supremely confident traders tend to sell off more exotic stocks on December 31 (D-day for performance reviews and bonus calculations) just so as not to deviate too far from the herd. Similary, fear of regret (known as endowment effect) prevents people from discarding items no longer necessary - fearing its regret repercussions should it turn out that you needed those worn-out tennis shoes after all!

Remorse can be particularly overwhelming when coupled with an "last chance" offer, such as safari brochures that claim they provide "your last opportunity to see a rhino before its species becomes extinct". But why would anyone fly all the way from Europe just now for such an irrational purpose?

So let's say you have long dreamt of owning your own home, yet land is becoming scarce and only a handful of plots with lake views remain; three have come and gone, leaving just one as your last chance! Feeling panic-stricken at what seems like being the last opportunity available, you buy this plot at an exorbitant price, believing this might be it; in reality though real estate with stunning lake views will continue appearing on the market; last chances can make us panic-stricken, leading us down this route - even for experienced deal makers!

See also Scarcity Error (ch. 27); Endowment Effect (ch. 23); Alternative Paths (ch. 39) and Framing (ch. 42

Imagine for a moment that marijuana has been the focus of mainstream media discourse for some time now, with television shows portraying potheads, clandestine growers and dealers; tabloid press printing photos of 12-year-old girls smoking joints; broadsheets exploring medical aspects as well as philosophical considerations of marijuana usage - everyone seems talking about it! Let's assume smoking does not adversely impact driving in any way - any driver could wind up involved in an accident at some point just by coincidence; similarly drivers with joint may end up involved in accidents from time to time just like anyone else - entirely by chance alone!

Kurt is a local journalist. One evening while driving home he comes upon an accident scene with a car wrapped around a tree trunk. Due to his relationship with local law enforcement he learns that they found marijuana hidden within the back seat of this car - prompting him to rush back to the newsroom with this headline: 'Marijuana Kills Yet Another Motorist'.

As previously discussed, we assume there is no statistical relationship between marijuana use and car accidents and their respective accidents, leaving Kurt's headline unjustified and his claims unsupported by facts. Kurt has fallen prey to something called the salience effect - in which prominent features or attributes gain more notice than they deserve; marijuana being such an obvious one here has caused him to believe this incident was caused by it.

Once Kurt enters business journalism, an important event occurs: one of the world's biggest companies has just announced it will promote a woman to CEO! Kurt, thrilled at this development, immediately launches into writing his commentary: the woman likely got promoted due to being female - when in reality this probably had nothing to do with gender (since men typically hold most top roles); had women leadership been considered so important by other companies already acting, these would likely have done so long ago; in this news story alone gender becomes prominent, thus earning extra weight from Kurt and his reader.

Journalists aren't alone when it comes to falling prey to the salience effect - we all are. Two men rob a store.
Nigerian immigrants rob a bank, are immediately arrested, and revealed as such upon interrogation by law enforcement officers shortly thereafter. While no particular ethnic group can be held disproportionately responsible for bank robberies, we still associate lawless Nigerian immigrants with bank robberies; it distorts our thinking; we assume they're lawless immigrants at it again! Likewise if an Armenian commits rape it's often blamed on them rather than other factors present among American's that exist among Americans rather than other factors present that exists within Americans that also contributes towards

prejudices being formed despite the vast majority living lawful lives being forgotten - we recalling particularly noteworthy incidents which involve immigrants as soon as we hear about something related to them and it usually starts off with striking negative incidents first!

The salience effect can shape both our perception of past events as well as how we envision the future. Daniel Kahneman and Amos Tversky discovered that we often place undue weight on salient information when forecasting, which may explain why investors react more strongly to sensational news (such as CEO dismissals) than less striking information such as long-term profit growth projections. Even professional analysts cannot always circumvent its influence.

Conclusion: Salient information has an outsized influence on our thoughts and actions. We tend to overlook slow-developing factors with long-term effects that we tend to neglect altogether. Don't be blinded by irregularities; for instance a book with an eye-catching, vibrant red jacket makes the bestseller list, prompting readers to attribute its success solely to its cover art - don't fall for this temptation: gather enough mental strength to fight seemingly obvious explanations!

See also The Halo Effect (ch. 38); Primacy and Recency Effects (ch. 73); Confirmation Bias (chs 7-8); Induction (ch 31); Fundamental Attribution Error (ch 36) and Affect Heuristic (ch 66)

WHY MONEY IS NOT NAKED.

One autumn day in the early 1980s was windy with wet leaves swirling about. Pushing my bike up the hill towards school, I noticed something odd at my feet: a large and rust-brown leaf was revealed as being worth 500 Swiss Franc bills - approximately $250 today; an absolute fortune at that time for a high school student! That money soon vanished from my pocket; I quickly used it towards purchasing one of the top models available with disc brakes and Shimano gears (although my previous bike worked fine!), even though my old bike still worked fine as before!

Though I wasn't completely penniless back then, having managed to save up a few hundred francs through mowing grass in my neighbourhood, the thought never crossed my mind to waste such hard-earned money on something so frivolous as going to movies or going shopping - my spending wasn't excessive and made more sense when reflecting upon this behavior; money may only be perceived differently depending on its source; therefore it comes with emotional associations attached that add extra layers.

Two questions. Let's imagine that after working hard for one year, and at its end you find that you have an additional $20,000 in your account than at its start, what would you do with it? A) Leave it sitting in your bank. B) Invest it. C) Use it for necessary improvements like renovating a moldy kitchen or replacing worn-out tires. D) Treat yourself to an extravagant cruise vacation.

As is typical for most people, you will likely choose A, B, or C as their answer.

Second question. What would you do if you won $20,000 in the lottery? Choose from A, B, C or D as above; most people now take either C or D which reveals flawed thinking; although you are free to count it however you please; $20,000 remains $20,000.

Casinos provide us with many examples of delusions similar to this. A friend places $1,000 on a roulette table - only to lose it all - then claims: 'I didn't gamble away $1,000; I won all that earlier.' When asked by others about his losses, he replies with: 'But it's the same amount!' and insists: 'Not at all!
'"Don't tell me!" He laughs. We treat money we win, discover or inherit with more carelessness than money earned through hard work; economist Richard Thaler termed this effect the house-money effect; it leads us to take greater risks; lottery winners often find themselves worse off once they cash their winnings; in this sense the old saying - win some, lose some - can only serve to minimize real losses.

Thaler split his students into two groups. One learned they had won $30 and could participate in a coin toss where tails meant $9 in returns, and heads would result in $9 losses; 7 out of 10 students decided to risk it and take part. By contrast, another group discovered they had won nothing at first glance, yet had an option between receiving $30 as promised or engaging in another coin toss where heads won $21 while tails netted $39. However, only 43% took up either option even though both options offered the same expected value: $30

Marketing strategists understand the power of the house-money effect. Online gambling sites'reward' you with $100 credit when signing up, credit card companies give free call credit when filling out applications forms, airlines give away miles when joining frequent flyer clubs and phone companies provide call credit to help people become accustomed to making calls more frequently - all thanks to this subtle strategy known as the house-money effect! Much of coupon craze stems from this phenomenon.

Conclusion: Be wary when winning money or getting something for free from a business. Chances are high that you'll pay it back with interest out of sheer exuberance; therefore it is better to strip any opulence off this apparent free money, convert it to workman's clothing, deposit it in your bank account, or put it back into your own company as quickly as possible.

See also: Endowment Effect, Scarcity Error and Loss Aversion in Chapter 23--32 for further analysis of resolutions that don't work (chp 23-25 and 32-33)

Procrastination

My friend is an artist; his books contain about 100 pages every seven years and produce two lines of print per day - at most! When questioned about his miserable productivity he replied 'Research is much more enjoyable than writing.' As such, he sits at his desk, surfing the web for hours on end or poring over obscure books in search of great and forgotten stories to write down before convincing himself it wouldn't make sense until he was in "the right mood". Unfortunately this happens rarely enough to justify procrastinating his writing as he convinced himself starting only once the "right mood" came along and took hold - rarely occurring!

Another friend has tried daily for the last ten years to stop smoking; each cigarette could be his final one. Meanwhile, my tax returns have been sitting unfinished on my desk for six months; though I haven't lost hope that they'll fill themselves out eventually.

Procrastination is the tendency to put off taking actions which require sacrifice - going to the gym, switching insurance policies for cheaper policies or writing thank-you letters are just a few examples of such tasks that may need doing and resolutions won't help in these instances.

Procrastination is folly, given that no task completes itself. We know they're useful so why do we put them off until another time? Because time lags between sowing and reaping. Psychology professor Roy Baumeister demonstrated this idea through a brilliant experiment. He set students in front of an oven full of chocolate cookies being baked, sending out their irresistibly fragrant aroma into the room. He then placed a bowl full of radishes near the oven, and instructed students that they could consume as many as they liked without restriction; cookies however were strictly off limits. He left them alone in the room for thirty minutes. Students in a second group were permitted to gorge freely on cookies before both groups attempted a difficult maths problem involving cookies; those forbidden from eating any dropped out twice as quickly than those allowed unlimited cookie consumption; this period of self-control had passed successfully.
Willpower was depleted, leaving them without enough mental energy or willpower to tackle the task at hand. Willpower acts like a battery; once depleted, future challenges could prove insurmountable.

Self-control cannot always be available all of the time; it needs time and space for rejuvenation. Luckily, all it takes to accomplish this goal is refuelling blood sugar and relaxing - two simple yet important strategies!

Though eating enough and taking regular breaks are essential components of success, the next crucial element is using various tricks to stay on the right path. This may involve eliminating distractions - for instance when writing novels I often disable Internet access so as not to become sidetracked when reaching a knotty part of writing. But the most powerful technique of all is setting deadlines; psychologist Dan Ariely found that external authorities - such as teachers or IRS officials - tend to work best. Self-imposed deadlines only work if the task has been broken down stepwise with each part receiving its own due date; hence this nebulous New Year resolutions doomed to failure!

Procrastination is both human and irrational; therefore, to combat it effectively use an integrated approach. My neighbor managed to write her doctoral thesis in three months using this strategy: renting a small room without telephone or Internet connectivity and setting three dates per part of her paper for each deadline she announced to anyone willing to listen (including printing them on her business cards!) She refueled herself during lunch time or evening hours by reading fashion magazines or sleeping.

See also: Omission Bias (ch. 44); Planning Fallacy (ch. 91); Action Bias (ch. 43); Hyperbolic Discounting (ch. 51); Zeigarnik Effect (ch. 93)

BUILD YOUR OWN CASTLE

Envy What would make you most jealous? There are three scenarios of envy which might irritate you: A) When your friends' salaries increase while yours remain the same. B) Their average salaries decrease while yours do. C) Your average salaries decrease and vice versa.

If your answer was A, do not worry: this is quite normal: just another victim of the green-eyed monster!

Here's a Russian tale: A farmer finds a magic lamp. After rubbing it, out of thin air comes an unnamed genie, promising them one wish. After thinking for some time and considering his options, the farmer finally decides: My neighbor has a cow; therefore I hope she dies so I may inherit hers'.

As absurd as it may sound, you likely can relate to the farmer. Admit it: similar thoughts must have crossed your mind at some point in life. Consider your colleague who earns a large bonus while you receive only a gift certificate: envy can lead to unwise actions such as refusing to help him anymore and even puncturing the tires of his Porsche; secretly delighting when his leg breaks skiing is an outcome you secretly rejoice over.

Envy stands out among all emotions as one that's easy to shake off, unlike anger, sadness, or fear. According to Balzac's analysis of envy as vice - for there is no single benefit it brings with it - envy can only serve one purpose - sincere flattery; otherwise it is time wasted. Envy can arise in many forms: ownership, status, health, youth talent popularity beauty. Because physical reactions of both are similar, envy can easily be mistaken for jealousy; the difference lies in what its subject is (status money health etc). For jealousy to occur it needs at least two parties involved while envy requires at least three (Peter is jealous that Sam doesn't answer his phone while the beautiful girl next door rings him instead).

Envy can often lead us down an unhealthy path by turning on those most similar to us in age, career and residence. But why do we feel resentment towards businesspeople from another century, plants or animals that do not pose threats or lack social status - none of this deserved envy in any case!
As a writer, I don't envy millionaires from across the world; rather those within my city. Musicians, managers or dentists come first. CEOs envy other large CEOs; supermodels envy more successful supermodels; as Aristotle said it best: 'Potters envy potters.'

Assume for example that your financial success allows you to relocate from one of New York's rougher neighbourhoods to Manhattan's Upper East Side. At first, this move may feel great; friends may admire your apartment and address. But quickly thereafter, you realize there are apartments of differing proportions around you, along with new peer groups made up of much richer individuals compared to your old peer group, causing new issues to surface - envy and status anxiety among them.

How can you combat envy? First, stop comparing yourself with others. Second, find your circle of competence and fill it on your own; carve out an area in which you shine - no matter how small - so that everyone knows that YOU are the master of that castle.

Like all emotions, envy has its roots in human evolution. If the hominid from the cave next door took more of the mammoth's meat than was fair for us losers, envy motivated us to do something about it; lax hunter-gatherers died of starvation while others feasted. Today however, envy no longer plays such an integral role. If my neighbor buys themselves a Porsche that doesn't mean any less for me!

When I feel my envy rise, my wife reminds me: 'It is OK to envy those whom you aspire to become.'

See also Social Comparison Bias (Ch. 72); Hedonic Treadmill (Ch. 46).

Personification For 18 years, American media was prohibited from showing photographs of fallen soldiers' coffins. When defence secretary Robert Gates lifted this ban in February 2009, images poured onto the Internet in their thousands. Officially, family members need to give approval before anything can be published; but in reality this rule cannot be enforced effectively. This restriction had one purpose - to cover up the true costs of war - by disguising their true numbers as statistics while real people evoke emotion in us all.

Why is this the case? For millennia, groups have been essential to our survival, so over the past 100,000 years we have developed an incredible ability to read other people's minds - this scientific term is known as 'the theory of mind'. Here's an experiment to demonstrate this: you are given $100 and must split it with someone, your suggestion being considered whether if he/she accepts your offer, the money is divided accordingly or returned back - should the other person not agree, you must return it all without getting anything back - how will this play out?

At first glance it would make sense to give an unknown stranger very little - such as just $1 - because anything would be better than nothing. Yet economists conducting experiments using ultimatum games (the technical term) observed subjects behaving quite differently when participating. They would offer between 30%-50%, anything below which was seen as unfair - an example of our empathy towards another human. The ultimatum game can serve as an eye opener into how our perceptions differ depending on who's looking out.

However, with one small modification it is possible to significantly diminish this feeling: moving players to separate rooms. When people can no longer see or have never met their counterparts - or have never known of them - simulating their feelings becomes much harder; eventually becoming an abstraction altogether and their share drops below 20% on average.

Paul Slovic conducted another experiment by soliciting donations. One group saw a picture of Rokia from Malawi - an undernourished child living on charity - before being shown her photo and being shown how much money would help.
After being shown statistics regarding Malawi's famine, people in one group donated on average $2.83 out of $5 they received to complete a brief survey; after being shown statistics detailing more than three million malnourished children being affected, average donations dropped 50%; this seemed counter-intuitive as one would think people's generosity would increase with knowing of its scale; unfortunately this does not seem to be the case; people not statistics drive our actions!

Media organizations have long recognized that boring factual reports and bar charts don't draw readers in; as a result, their guideline for reporting stories has long been to give each event an "image". When reporting about a company or state featured in the news, for example, a picture of its CEO usually appears alongside it (either grinning or grimacing depending on market demand), with state presidents or governors becoming icons within these stories; when something like an earthquake strikes, its victims become the face of it all.

This obsession explains the success of one of culture's great inventions: the novel. This literary "killer app" projects individual and interpersonal conflicts onto individual destinies. Instead of an academic writing an exhaustive dissertation about psychological torture in Puritan New England, we still read Hawthorne's The Scarlet Letter; similarly for The Great Depression? While its statistics may seem distant to most of us, as experienced through Steinbeck's The Grapes of Wrath it remains vivid in memory.

Conclusion: Be wary when encountering human stories. Inquire into their facts and statistical distribution so you can better contextualize their narrative. If you wish to move or motivate people for your own ends, however, ensure your tale includes names and faces as this will make for more powerful storytelling.

See also Story Bias (ch. 13); News Illusion (ch. 99); Linking Bias (ch. 22)

After heavy rainfall in southern England, a river overflowed its banks. Police closed and diverted traffic at its crossing for two weeks - yet at least once each day at least one car drove past warning signs and into the swift-flowing water, completely unaware of what lay directly before them.

Harvard psychologists Daniel Simons and Christopher Chabris conducted an experiment in which two teams of students passed a basketball back and forth between teams wearing black or white T-shirts - with black wearing black T-shirts being more efficient at passing balls back than their counterparts in passing them backwards. This short clip known as "The Monkey Business Illusion" can be viewed online (watch it before reading more!). Take a look here before reading further!) Viewers are asked to count how often players in white T-shirts pass the ball between both teams as they weave through circles weaving in and out and passing back and forth. At one point in the video, something unexpected occurred: a student dressed as a gorilla suddenly entered and began pounding his chest before quickly departing again. You are asked at the end if you noticed anything unusual; half of viewers responded in disbelief that there had even been any strange behavior; they couldn't comprehend any such presence - surely no gorilla is present here?

The Monkey Business Test is one of the most well-known experiments in psychology and highlights what psychologists call an illusion of attention: we think we notice everything happening around us when in reality we tend to only notice what we are concentrating on - here, the passes made by Team White; unannounced interruptions can even be as large and conspicuous as a gorilla!

At times, making phone calls while driving can put our perception of attention at risk. Most times this does not present any issues; making calls generally has no adverse impact on driving tasks such as keeping within lanes and applying brakes when necessary. But once something unexpected occurs - like a child running across the road - your attention becomes stretched too thin to react appropriately in time; studies show this to be true with either cell phones or alcohol being involved.
No matter how you hold or use a phone, its impact on your response time to unexpected events remains limited.

Do you recognise the phrase, 'The elephant in the room?' This refers to an obvious topic that no one wants to discuss; an unspoken taboo. By contrast, we could define "The gorilla in the room" as: an issue which must be discussed immediately but is being overlooked or disregarded because nobody knows about it.

Swissair was an airline so focused on expansion that it ignored its rapidly diminishing liquidity, leading to its bankruptcies in 2001 and 2002. Or consider mismanagement within Eastern Bloc nations that led to their separation, leading to Berlin Wall falling and risks on banks' books which nobody cared much about prior to 2007. These examples show us just how often gorillas roam among us without us realizing.

Not every extraordinary event escapes us; rather, what we fail to notice goes unheeded and goes unseen by us; thus leaving us unaware of any significant items we are overlooking and giving rise to the false belief that everything of importance is being observed by us.

Every now and then, free yourself of the illusion of attention. Think through all possible and seemingly improbable scenarios - unexpected events may arise that nobody is talking about; lurking issues no one addresses are not being addressed; be vigilant of silence as much as noise; check peripheral areas instead of just central ones; anticipate something unusual but huge - being huge doesn't guarantee being noticed; something unusual must also be expected to appear!

See also: Feature-Positive Effect (ch. 95); Confirmation Bias (chs 7-8), Availability Bias (ch 11) and Primacy and Recency Effects (ch 73)

Imagine applying for your dream job: you polish up your resume until it sparkles, shine during an interview, and highlight all of your achievements and abilities while downplaying any weaknesses or setbacks. When they ask if you could boost sales by 30% while cutting costs by 30%, your response should be: 'Consider it done." Regardless of any concerns inside you about how this might happen, focus on impressing interviewers first; the details will follow later; any attempts at providing non-fantasy answers could potentially put yourself out of contention and ultimately result in disqualifying you from further consideration by interviewers; give even semi-realistic answers that could put yourself out of consideration - no matter how good they sound in return.

Imagine yourself as a journalist with an outstanding book idea that everyone is talking about. After finding an interested publisher willing to pay an advance, he asks when can he expect the manuscript (can it be ready in six months?) You stammer: 'Hmm... No idea. How long did it take me last time?" You answer with: 'Consider it done.' Once the contract is signed and money in your bank account, there's always time for other projects and writing stories!

Strategic misrepresentation is the official term for such behavior: the higher the stakes are, the more exaggerated your assertions should become. Although strategic misrepresentation won't work everywhere - for instance if an eye doctor promises five consecutive times to give you perfect vision only to deliver worse-than-before results after each procedure, eventually you may stop believing his promises altogether - strategic misrepresentation might still prove valuable when trying one-time efforts, such as interviews (where one company won't hire you more than once!). However it shouldn't work here either; instead it might well work when faced with only once-off attempts or unique attempts involving unique attempts - something an ophthalmologist wouldn't.

Mega-projects are particularly susceptible to misrepresentation when their accountability is diffuse, such as when government which originally funded them no longer holds power, many businesses participate and often point fingers, or the end date is some years off. Bent Flyvbjerg of Oxford knows large-scale projects intimately. Cost and schedule overruns are common because winning offers don't always reflect overall excellence; rather it comes down to what looks best on paper - something Flyvbjerg calls 'reverse Darwinism': the one producing the most hot air will usually win out. Is strategic misrepresentation simply deceptive practice? Not necessarily; just as women wearing makeup is deceitful while men leasing Porsches to show financial prowes is deceptive - deceitful but socially acceptable so we don't get upset by it - same goes with misrepresentation practices used when women wear make-up or men leasing Porsches to show financial prowess are objectively deceived but socially acceptable so we don't get upset by it either! Same holds true with strategic misrepresentation schemes used during negotiations - even if only one party knows about misrepresentation tactics used against another party but can get away with being misrepresented during negotiations; same counts when applied strategically misrepresentation can get away with being disreputable when applied in terms of deceiveness when applied strategically as well - like men leasing Porsches as signal financial prowess to signal financial prowess are simply lying in this regard liamousness but don't get upset by socially acceptable so we don't get worked up about strategic misrepresentation. The same holds true of strategic misrepresentation used against them both deceptionfully used against one or the other than expected or treated differently depending upon. The same with misrepresented when used when misrepresented lither.

Strategic misrepresentation may not always have serious repercussions; however, when it comes to matters that truly matter such as your health or future employees, be wary. When dealing with people (whether candidates for office, authors or ophthalmologists), don't rely on what they claim; look at their past performance instead. When dealing with projects (be they similar projects or new proposals that seem unrealistically optimistic). Be wary of any that seem unrealistically optimistic; ask an accountant to scrutinize plans thoroughly; add a clause into contracts that stipulates penalties should they occur; and transfer this money directly into an escrow account to safeguard its safe keeping escrow account as an added measure against cost overruns.

See also Overconfidence Effect (ch. 15) for details and where is the off switch.

OVERTHINKING

There was once an intelligent centipede who sat idly by an edge of a table when they noticed a delectable grain of sugar across the room. He quickly assessed his options: which table leg should he crawl up or down on first? Next he had to determine who should take the first step and in which order. Since he was adept with maths he conducted all necessary calculations and chosen one path over all others before finally taking its initial step. Unfortunately though his calculation and contemplation caused him tangle up in midair which caused him to stop dead before further progress could have been achieved; in effect starved him and eventually starved him out before ever making progress could have been reached and starved out before ever getting closer or further along in life than ever imagined before and died starved out due to overthinking.

At the 1999 British Open golf tournament, French golfer Jean Van de Velde played flawlessly up until the final hole, where he led by three shots. Even with that three-shot advantage he could comfortably afford two over par shots without falling short; making entry to the big leagues only moments away! As Van de Velde stepped onto the course, beads of sweat began forming on his forehead. His first swing ended up flying into the bushes twenty feet from its target hole and made Van de Velde increasingly nervous for subsequent shots which only served to increase this sensation of anxiety. Van de Velde hit his ball into knee-high grass before dropping it in the water, taking off his shoes to wade through. For a moment he considered shooting from the pond; eventually though he decided on taking a penalty shot into sand; after shooting into it seven times it finally made its way onto the green and into its hole; Van de Velde lost the British Open but secured himself a place in sporting history through this now-famous triple-bogey performance.

Consumer Reports conducted a tasting experiment with experienced tasters in the 1980s, involving 45 varieties of strawberry jelly. Later, psychology professors Timothy Wilson and Jonathan Schooler conducted similar tests using University of Washington students; similar results emerged, with both experts and students favoring similar flavors of jelly. But Wilson went further: He conducted another test with another group of students who preferred different ones than before - only this time they chose different options altogether!
In the first group, participants filled out a lengthy questionnaire justifying their ratings in detail and came up with completely lopsided rankings, featuring some of the finest varieties at the bottom.

Fundamentally, too much thinking impedes one's access to the wisdom of your emotions. Although this statement might seem unusual coming from someone like myself who strives to clear away irrationality from my thinking processes, emotions form just like crystal-clear rational thoughts; emotions simply represent a different form of information processing which may provide wiser advice than rational ones.

This leads to an important question: when should one listen to their head or their gut? Rule of thumb might include this: when it comes to activities like motor skills (centipede, Van de Velde or learning a musical instrument) and questions you have addressed many times before (such as Warren Buffett's "circle of competence"), it is best not to overanalyze too closely. Deliberative decision-making undermines your intuitive abilities to address problems. Just as in Stone Age times, when making food-related and friendship decisions, so-called heuristics were superior to rational thought. With complex matters such as investment decisions requiring sober reflection though, evolution did not equip us for such considerations, so logic always outshines intuition.

See also Action Bias (Ch. 43); Information Bias (Ch. 59)

WHY YOU TAKE ON TOO MUCH DEBT (Chapter 91).

Planning Fallacy

Every morning when making your to-do list, do you often achieve success at ticking everything off at the end of each day? How often is this the case for most people? Most may only reach this state once every few months. Simply put, you take on too much. Your plans are unrealistically ambitious - something which would be forgiven had this been your first time compiling to-do lists, but this behavior has become part of your routine over time. Thus, you're intimately acquainted with your capabilities and are unlikely to overestimate them daily. This is no laughing matter: in other areas of life we learn from experience - why isn't there one when it comes to planning? Even though most of your previous endeavors were too optimistic for reality today. Daniel Kahneman refers to this phenomenon as the planning fallacy.

Roger Buehler and his research team asked their final-year class, led by Canadian psychologist Roger Buehler, to identify two submission dates: one was realistic while the second reflected an unlikely worst-case scenario scenario date. Only 30% met realistic deadlines while they typically needed 50% extra time than originally planned and an extra seven days than anticipated for submission dates set under worst case scenarios.

The planning fallacy is particularly evident when people collaborate, be it in business, science or politics. Groups tend to overestimate duration and benefits while underestimating costs and risks systematically. A prime example is Sydney Opera House which was planned in 1957 with completion anticipated in 1963 at an initial estimated cost of $7 million but eventually opened for business at $102 million; 14 times higher than expected!

Why don't we seem natural planners? There may be two reasons for our ineffective planning abilities. One is wishful thinking: We strive for success in everything we take on. Two: Too often, we focus too intently on our project while neglecting outside influences such as unexpected events that arise unexpectedly (this could happen with daily schedules too, e.g. your daughter wanting something) which then lead us down an unpredictable path; or too little attention given to these events due to being focused too narrowly on them (this might even apply here - when planning).
Your dog swallows a fish bone. Your car battery quits on you unexpectedly. An offer for a house appears and needs urgent consideration on your desk - plans go awry as a result! Would step-by-step preparation be any solution? No; step-by-step preparation only magnifies planning fallacies by narrowing focus further, thus decreasing your ability to anticipate surprises in life.

So what should you do? Shift your focus from internal things - like your project - to external ones such as similar projects. Review the base rate and assess past efforts. If similar ventures lasted three years and consumed $5 million, that will likely apply to your project as well - no matter how carefully planned. Therefore, before making decisions for any decisions related to it are made it's crucial that a "premortem" session (literally meaning, "before death") be performed prior to making these important choices. Gary Klein suggests giving this short speech to any assembled team: 'Imagine it is one year later and that everything went according to plan but in its place there has been disaster - take five or ten minutes writing about this catastrophe - stories will show you how things may develop."

See also Procrastination (ch. 85); Forecast Illusion (ch. 40); Zeigarnik Effect (ch. 93); Groupthink (ch. 25) for more.

WILDERING HAMMERS ONLY SEE NAILS

PROFESSIONAL DEFORMATION SYSTEM

An individual takes out a loan and launches his own company only to declare bankruptcy shortly afterwards.

He experiences depression and then commits suicide.

Are You Reading this Story as a Business Analyst? As such, as part of your job you should attempt to assess why this idea didn't succeed: Was he an ineffective leader, the strategy wrong, the market too small, or competition too fierce? As a marketer, you may assume the campaigns were poorly organized or that he failed to reach his intended audience. Financial experts may question if the loan is the appropriate financial instrument; local journalists see an opportunity in this story: how fortunate that he took his own life! As a writer, you might muse over how an incident could become an ancient Greek tragedy. Bankers might suspect an error occurred in loan department. Socialists tend to blame capitalism's failure; religious conservatives might view this event as divine punishment or psychiatrists would recognize low serotonin levels. So which viewpoint should prevail?

None. Mark Twain once observed, 'If all your tools are hammers, all your problems will be nails.' Charlie Munger, Warren Buffett's business partner and author of The Snowball Effect remarked to Charlie Munger the following effect of using only one model: 'But this can be an entirely disastrous way of thinking and operating in the world; therefore multiple models must come from different fields as not all wisdom lies within one single academic department'

Here are a few examples of deformation professionelle: surgeons seek to solve every medical problem with surgery; armies tend to favor military solutions first; engineers specialize in structural work; trend gurus often make absurd predictions - in short: when asked about an issue, most answers usually relate to one of their areas of expertise.

Why shouldn't tailors practice tailoring as they know best? Deformation professionnelle occurs when people apply their specialized processes in areas they shouldn't. No doubt you have seen it happen yourself?
Teachers scolding friends like students. New mothers treating their husbands like children. Or take Excel spreadsheets - we use them even when their use doesn't make any sense, such as when projecting financial projections for startups or comparing potential lovers we found

via dating sites - they may very well be one of the most dangerous inventions since computers.

Even within their own domains, literary reviewers tend to overuse the hammer. Reviewers are trained to detect references, symbols and hidden messages within books; as a novelist myself, I find this practice irritating as reviewers conjure such devices where none exist. Not unlike what business journalists do - who scour even minor comments made by central bank governors for any hint of fiscal policy changes through parsing of words spoken aloud by them.

Conclusion: When consulting an expert, do not expect an overall best solution; expect rather an approach which can be solved using their toolbox. Remember that our minds are not centralised computers but instead contain multiple specialized tools which may need to be employed at various points along their journey. Unfortunately, our "pocketknives" are incomplete. Due to life experiences and professional expertise, we already own some blades. But in order to hone our skill set further, it is necessary to add two or three tools - mental models which fall outside our area of expertise - into our toolbox. Over the past several years, I've adopted a biological perspective on life and gained new insight into complex systems. Take stock of your deficiencies and seek appropriate knowledge and methodologies to address them; doing so takes about one year of effort but will pay dividends: your pocketknife will become bigger and more versatile, your mind sharper!

See also Volunteer's Folly (ch. 65); Domain Dependence (ch. 76) and Gambler's Fallacy (ch. 29)

MISSION ACCOMPLISHED

ZEIGARNIK EFFECT

Berlin, 1927: Several university students and professors visit a restaurant where the waiter takes order after order with no documentation being written down, worrying them that something bad will surely happen. However, after only a short wait all diners received exactly what they requested. Outside on the street after dinner however, Russian psychology student Bluma Zeigarnik realized she had left her scarf behind at the restaurant. Back at the restaurant, she encounters the waiter renowned for his incredible memory and asks if he has seen it. However, he remains unaware of her or where she had sat; to which she responds indignantly by asking how it was possible he forgot who or where they sat when his memory is so incredible! 'How could you forget me?" she demands, incredulous at his lack of awareness. His response: 'I keep every order in my head until it is served' he replied curtly: 'I keep every order in my head until served' he replied curtly: 'I keep every order until served' 'The waiter replied curtly: 'I keep every order in my head until served' and didn't remember my previous orders either' (c).

Zeigarnik and Kurt Lewin studied this mysterious behavior and concluded that people generally function like waiters: we never forget unfinished tasks; they nag at our consciousness until we give them attention; once completed however, these items disappear from memory altogether.

Researchers now refer to this phenomenon as the Zeigarnik effect. Her investigation, however, unearthed some unusual instances: for instance some individuals remained completely unstressed despite having multiple projects underway. Roy Baumeister and his research team at Florida State University recently shed some light on this phenomenon. He divided students who were close to taking their final examinations into three groups; Group 1 consisted of parties held during this semester while Groups 2-4 focused on formal examinations. Group 2 had to focus on their upcoming exam while group 3 needed to create a detailed study plan. Baumeister then asked students in Groups 2, 3 and 4 to complete words under time pressure - some saw "Panic", while others thought of 'Party" or Paris. This exercise proved extremely insightful; group 1 appeared relaxed about taking their exam while those in groups 2 could think of nothing else! However, what really stood out was group 3, where their results were truly astonishing!
Although these students had to focus on an upcoming exam, their minds remained relaxed and free from anxiety. Subsequent experiments verified this observation: outstanding tasks tend to gnaw at us only until we have an organized plan of how we will address them; Zeigarnik mistakenly believed completing tasks would suffice in this regard; instead a strategic approach should suffice.

David Allen's best-selling book Getting Things Done (GTD) proclaims his goal as one of having a mind as clear as water. To achieve this goal, one does not need a life in perfect order but must create an action plan to address life's unplanned issues and write them down in step-by-step tasks - only then can your mind find peace of mind. Deliberateness in planning is paramount; vague goals like 'organise my wife's birthday party" or "finding new employment" cannot provide relief; Allen forces his clients to break these projects down into twenty to fifty individual tasks before commencing such projects if possible in order to ensure success and achieve peace of mind.

Allen's recommendation may run counter to the planning fallacy (chapter 91): detailed planning can cause us to overlook factors from outside that can derail projects, but therein lies the key: for peace of mind opt for Allen's approach while for more accurate estimates on costs, benefits, duration and other project aspects look up similar projects instead of creating one detailed plan. Or do both!

However, you don't need any high-tech gadgets to accomplish this yourself - simply keep a notepad by your bed and use it when you can't sleep to write down outstanding tasks and how you will address them - this should help silence inner voices that keep calling out: 'you want God but have no cat food left," as Allen put it - his advice remains valid even if you already found God or don't own any pets!

See also Procrastination (ch. 85); Planning Fallacy (ch. 91) for additional considerations.

Boat Construction Is More Crucial than Rowing

Why Are So Few Serial Entrepreneurs

Why do there seem to be so few serial entrepreneurs - businesspeople who start multiple profitable companies consecutively? Sure, Steve Jobs and Richard Branson exist - they represent a small minority though. Serial entrepreneurs account for less than one per cent of all startup founders. But do these serial entrepreneurs all retire to private yachts after experiencing success, like Microsoft co-founder Paul Allen did? No way. True business people possess too much energy to just sit around on a beach chair for hours on end. Perhaps this is due to them not wanting to let go and cosset their firms until they turn 65, although most founders sell off their shares within 10 years of founding their companies. One would think that people endowed with talent, an expansive personal network, and solid credentials would be capable of founding numerous other start-ups - yet many do not succeed at doing so. Why do they stop? They didn't stop; they just failed at doing so successfully. Luck plays a larger role than skill when it comes to business success, which no businessperson likes hearing about. I remember feeling uncomfortable when first learning of this idea; my immediate thought was: 'Was my success just random?". At first it may feel offensive that luck has played such a large part.

Let's take an honest, realistic approach to business success. How much of it comes down to hard work and distinct talent vs luck? Unfortunately, this question can easily lead to misperceptions; while talent plays an essential part in any company's success story, hard work cannot achieve results alone. Unfortunately, neither skills nor hard work alone are enough to achieve success; both elements are necessary - but not sufficient - factors. How can we know this? There is an easy and straightforward test: when someone enjoys long-term success compared to less qualified peers, talent becomes paramount. Unfortunately this does not apply to company founders; otherwise most successful entrepreneurs would continue launching multiple startups after the initial success was attained.

What role do corporate leaders play in the success of a company? Researchers identified traits associated with being a strong CEO - management procedures and prior strategic brilliance as examples.
Researchers then measured the correlation between CEO behaviors on one hand, and company value growth under their tenure on the other hand. Their conclusion: If two companies are randomly compared, in 60% of cases the stronger CEO leads the more powerful firm. Kahneman found that in 40% of cases, weaker CEOs led stronger companies; this represented only 10 percentage points more than no relationship at all. He concluded by noting how people generally don't enthusiastically buy books written about business leaders who are only slightly better than average on average; even Warren Buffett

doesn't see any sense in elevating certain CEOs; his take? '[?...?] A good managerial record depends more upon which boat one enters than on how effectively one steers it'

Certain areas don't rely on skill at all. Kahneman described in his book Thinking, Fast and Slow his visit to an asset management firm which sent a spreadsheet with each adviser's performance over eight years as part of their briefing for him. Out of this data, Kahneman assigned each group a ranking: 1, 2, 3 etc in descending order. He quickly calculated their relationship across years' rankings. He then calculated the correlation of rankings from year 1 through year 8 - with advisers occasionally being at either end. It turned out to be pure random chance; at times they would even appear nearer the top than at times the bottom. Adviser performance was independent from prior or subsequent years - the correlation was zero! And yet these consultants received bonuses for their accomplishment. In other words, the company was rewarding luck over skill.

Conclusion: Certain professions rely heavily on people using their abilities, such as pilots, plumbers and lawyers. Other areas require skill but it's not critical - like entrepreneurs and leaders. And sometimes chance decides everything, like in financial markets; here, the illusion of skill can reign supreme. So show respect to plumbers while enjoying successful financial jesters!
See also Beginner's Luck (ch. 49); Survivorship Bias (ch. 1), Authority Bias (ch. 9), Overconfidence Effect, Illusion of Control and Outcome Bias in subsequent chapters (20 and 21 respectively.

At first glance, series A appears simple enough. All its numbers share something in common - 394, 411, 054, 646 are linked by four features, which makes this series relatively straightforward to solve. Next comes series B; all its numbers utilize six features at some point. What can you learn from this? Absence can often be harder to detect than presence; we tend to place greater importance on things that exist rather than what does not.

Last week while out for a walk, it dawned on me: nothing hurt. This was quite surprising given I rarely experience pain anyway and when it occurs it can be intensely felt; yet rarely acknowledge its absence; such was its beauty that for just an instant it brought joy - only for it all to quickly slip from mind again!

At a classical recital, an orchestra performed Beethoven's Ninth Symphony to great acclaim in an enthusiastic concert hall. Tears could be seen welling up during its fourth movement ode, making one feel thankful it exists; but is that true? No doubt not; had the work not been composed, no one would miss it and the director wouldn't receive angry calls demanding that this piece of art be written and performed immediately - this phenomenon known as feature-positive effect is what really makes us happy today.

Prevention campaigns utilise this strategy effectively; for instance, "Smoking causes lung cancer" is far more persuasive than "Not smoking leads to a life free from lung cancer". Auditors and other professionals who rely on checklists often succumb to this feature-positive effect: outstanding tax declarations appear immediately in their lists while fraudulent activities such as those at Enron or Bernie Madoff's Ponzi scheme don't. Also missing from such lists are undertakings of "rogue traders", such as Nick Leeson and Jerome Kerviel who caused financial vagaries such as these - thus hiding such activities from public scrutiny.
No checklist exists to track devaluations; and while illegal acts might come under consideration by mortgage banks, devaluation due to incineration plants can occur without their monitoring being noticed.

Imagine creating an undesirable product like salad dressing with an elevated cholesterol content, but you want consumers to feel secure about its use? When labeling such a product, highlight all of its positive characteristics instead. Customers won't notice its absence; while positive features will ensure that consumers remain informed.

Academic research frequently exhibits the feature-positive effect. Confirmation of hypotheses typically leads to publications and can even earn Nobel prizes; while falsification of hypotheses, although scientifically beneficial, is much harder to publish and has never received this kind of prestigious acknowledgement. Another result of the feature-positive effect is our tendency towards accepting positive advice - such as doing X - over negative advice (forget Y). This makes us much more receptive towards positive advice than negative suggestions (such as forgetting Y).

Conclusion: Human beings often struggle to perceive non-events accurately. We tend to ignore what does not exist. For instance, we recognize if there is war but do not appreciate its absence during peacetime; similarly we rarely consider being sick when healthy; similarly after arriving in Cancun without having experienced a plane crash! By cultivating more mindfulness around absence we might well become happier; though doing this requires hard mental work and thought - one useful tool being questioning why something exists rather than nothingness as this question serves as a useful way of fighting feature positive effects!

See also Forer Effect (ch. 64); Confirmation Bias (chs. 7-8); Self-Selection Bias (ch. 47); Availability Bias (ch 11); Illusion of Attention (ch 88)

CONFIRMATION BIAS BETWEEN ARROW AND SPARROW

Cherry-Picking

Hotels present themselves in their best light online. Photos that portray beautiful, majestic images are carefully selected; any unflattering angles, leaky pipes or unattractive breakfast rooms are simply hidden by tattered carpeting - of course you know this to be true when faced with an unsightly lobby for the first time; instead you simply shrug and move towards registration desk as quickly as possible.

Cherry-picking, as practiced by hotels, involves selecting and emphasizing only attractive features while concealing others. You should approach other experiences similarly: brochures for cars, real estate or law firms are something else you need to approach with caution - knowing how they work doesn't ensnare us in their trance!

But you tend to respond differently when reading annual reports of companies, foundations and government organisations. Here you tend to expect objective depictions; unfortunately you'd be wrong: these bodies often cherry-pick: goals achieved are celebrated while setbacks go unremarked upon.

Imagine yourself as the head of a department. Your board invites you to present on your team's state of play. How would you approach this presentation? By emphasizing its victories while including some slides that highlight challenges. Any unmet achievements are easily forgotten about.

Anecdotes present a unique challenge when it comes to cherry-picking. Imagine being the MD of a company that manufactures technical devices. After conducting a customer satisfaction survey, it becomes apparent that most customers cannot use your gadget due to its complex nature. Now the HR manager chimes in: 'My father-in-law got this yesterday and immediately learned how to work it. How much weight would you assign this particular cherry? Close to zero." Refuting an anecdote can be challenging because it involves mini-stories that appeal to our brains. To counter this effect, skilled leaders train themselves throughout their careers to become hypersensitive to anecdotes that come their way and respond immediately with shots fired against any such stories that arise.
Cherry-picking becomes more apparent as we become immersed in more elevated or elite fields. In Antifragile, Taleb details how all areas of research - from philosophy to medicine and economics - boast of their results: "Like politicians, academia is adept at telling us what they did for us instead of what didn't; thus proving their indispensable methods." This may well be cherry-picking but our respect for academics makes this impossible for us to detect.

Or consider the medical profession: telling people not to smoke is the greatest medical achievement since World War II ended, according to physician Druin Burch in his book Taking the Medicine. A few cherry-like antibiotics serve as distractions and thus drug researchers tend to be celebrated while anti-smoking activists don't.

Administrative departments at large companies tend to behave like hoteliers by glorifying themselves by touting all that they've accomplished but never communicating what hasn't been accomplished for the business. What can you do about this? When serving on the supervisory board of an organization, be sure to ask about 'leftover cherries' such as failed projects or missed goals - you will learn much more from these than from successes! It is surprising how rarely such questions are brought up! Second: Instead of employing an army of financial controllers to calculate costs down to the last cent, take time to review targets regularly. You might be amazed to find that, over time, some original goals have become less tangible and have been replaced with self-imposed goals that remain always obtainable; any time such targets arise they should raise red flags; it would be the equivalent of shooting an arrow and creating a bull's-eye around where it lands!

Notes on Biases (ch. 13); Self-Serving Biases (ch. 45);

THE STONE-AGE HUNT FOR SCAPEGOATS

FAILURE OF SINGLE CAUSE ANALYSIS

Chris Matthews is one of MSNBC's premier journalists. On his news show, political experts are interviewed. I never understood what their job entailed or why such careers exist, though in 2003 the U.S. invasion of Iraq was front and center. Chris Matthews asked expert after expert about its motives - from 9/11 payback theories to weapons of mass destruction being behind this conflict - so important were his questions: 'What is the motivation for war? ', to "why did we invade Iraq, besides sales pitches." And on and so forth... and so forth... and so forth... and so forth...

Questions such as this no longer sit well with me; they reflect one of the most frequently occurring mental errors - something for which there is no everyday term; thus I will use awkward language like "the fallacy of single cause" instead.

Five years later, in 2008, panic reigned again in the financial markets and banks collapsed, forcing taxpayers to bail them out with tax dollars. Investors, politicians and journalists investigated every aspect of this financial meltdown: Greenspan's loose monetary policy? Investor stupidity? Dubious rating agencies? Corrupt auditors? Bad risk models or sheer greed were all possible causes - all were blameworthy in equal measure. No single factor can claim sole responsibility but all can contribute significantly.

An idyllic Indian summer, a friend's divorce, the First World War, cancer, a school shooting, the worldwide success of a company or even writing itself are events caused by multiple factors that contribute to them - yet we still try to pin all blame on one individual or thing alone.

What causes an apple to ripen and fall is not clear: is it gravity drawing it toward the earth, is its stem withering under sunlight's drying rays, that its weight has increased, that wind gusts cause its toppling or that an eager child standing underneath wants to snack on it? No single factor accounts for its falling.' In War and Peace by Tolstoy this passage illustrates this beautifully.

Imagine being the product manager for an iconic breakfast cereal brand and having recently introduced an organic, low-sugar variety that proves an overwhelming failure after one month of sales. How would you go about investigating its causes? Firstly, understand that no single factor will account for this failure; every factor plays its own part. Take a sheet of paper and sketch out all potential reasons, along with their root causes. When finished, you will have created an elaborate network of potential influencers. Next, identify those you can change (such as human nature) while discarding any that cannot. Finally, conduct empirical tests by varying highlighted factors across markets - this takes time and money but it is necessary if we wish to move beyond superficial assumptions.

The fallacy of single causation is both ancient and dangerous. Over the millennia we have come to believe that people are the masters of their own destinies - Aristotle made this claim more than two millennia ago! Now we understand this is incorrect and that free will is an open question. Our actions are determined by a complex web of factors ranging from genetic predisposition and environment, education, hormone concentration within brain cells and still we cling firmly to an outdated image of self-governance. This practice is both harmful and morally questionable. So long as we believe in singular reasons for events or disasters, it will always be possible to pin blame on individuals. Furthermore, people have long played this game of finding someone or something they blame - creating the perception that power must be exercised through one individual or group over another.

Yet Tracy Chapman was able to build her entire worldwide success on it - particularly through the song, 'Give Me One Reason.' But weren't there other factors involved as well?

See Also 'Because' Justification (ch. 52); Falsification of History (ch. 78); Hindsight Bias (ch. 14) and Fundamental Attribution Error (ch. 36) for further explanation.

INTENTION-TO-TREAT ERROR

While it might be hard to believe, speed demons actually drive more safely than so-called 'careful' drivers. Consider this: from Miami to West Palm Beach lies approximately 75 miles. Drivers covering a distance in under an hour we classify as reckless because their average speed exceeds 75mph; all others fall into our group of careful drivers. Which group experiences less accidents? It would have to be the reckless drivers. All three drivers completed the journey within an hour and, therefore, should not have been involved in any accidents; any who did find themselves in accidents automatically fall into the category of slower drivers. This example exemplifies an insidious fallacy referred to as intention-to-treat error that unfortunately lacks an attractive name.

This might sound similar to survivorship bias (chapter 1), but there is an important difference. With survivorship bias you only see successful projects or cars involved in accidents while with intention-to-treat error these failed projects or cars appear prominently but simply under an inappropriate category.

Recently, I was shown an eye-opening study conducted by a banker which revealed an interesting fact: companies with debt on their balance sheets tend to be significantly more profitable than firms that only hold equity as financial instruments (i.e. no debt on balance sheet). The banker insisted that every company should borrow at will, with his bank being the best place for this purpose. I examined his study more closely. How could that possibly be? From 1,000 randomly chosen firms, those receiving large loans produced higher returns both on equity and total capital than independently funded firms. They were all round more successful. Realization soon came: unprofitable companies do not qualify for corporate loans and thus fall into an "equity-only" group, where firms with larger cash cushions tend to stay afloat longer and remain part of this study despite any health problems they might present. On the other hand, firms that borrow heavily tend to fail more quickly. When they can no longer repay the interest on their debts, banks take over and sell off these businesses; those remaining within the "debt group" tend to remain relatively healthy regardless of how much debt is on their balance sheets.

Be wary if you think you understand. Recognizing intention-to-treat error can be challenging; let's use medicine as an example: A pharmaceutical company has created a new drug to combat heart disease. A study 'proves' this medication significantly reduces patients' mortality rates compared to taking placebo pills alone; among regular users the five-year mortality rate drops from 15% to 11% within five years, and two times higher among irregular users who took it in different amounts; so could it really be considered successful or fail?

Problematic is that pills may not be the determining factor; rather it's patient behavior that ultimately matters. Maybe patients discontinued due to severe side effects and found themselves in the "irregular intake" category or were too sick to continue regularly taking it; either way, only relatively healthy individuals remained within the "regular intake" group, making the drug appear far more effective than it really is; those truly sick patients who couldn't take regular doses were the ones populating the "irregular intake" cohorts.

Reputable studies allow medical researchers to analyze data of all the patients they initially intended to treat; no matter whether or not they took part in the trial. Unfortunately, however, many studies ignore this rule either intentionally or accidentally; be on guard: Always verify whether test subjects - drivers involved in accidents, bankrupt companies and critically ill patients have for some reason vanished from your sample population and file the study where it belongs: in the trashcan.

See also: Survivorship Bias (ch. 1); Will Rogers Phenomenon (ch. 58);

News Illusion Earthquake in Sumatra. Plane crash in Russia. Man holds daughter captive in cellar for 30 years; Heidi Klum splits with Seal; record salaries at Bank of America; attack in Pakistan; resignation of Mali's President; new world record in shot put throw.

Do you really require this knowledge?

We are extraordinarily well informed, yet remain very ignorant. That is because two centuries ago we invented a toxic form of knowledge called news that appeals to the mind like sugar does to the body - delicious yet potentially destructive over time.

Three years ago, I conducted an experiment. I quit reading and listening to news and cancelled all newspaper and magazine subscriptions; television and radio channels were cut from my lineup; news apps from my iPhone were deleted altogether. At first it was difficult, as I felt constantly anxious that something important might slip through my grasp; but after some time had passed I developed a different outlook. Three years later, my efforts paid off with clearer thoughts, deeper insights, better decisions and much more free time. Best of all - nothing important was missed due to my real-world social network acting as an information filter and keeping me up-to-date.

First of all, our brains react disproportionately to various types of information: scandalous, shocking details stimulate us; abstract, complex or unprocessed details have little effect. News producers understand this dynamic perfectly - their gripping stories, garish images and sensational 'facts' capture our attention while advertisers purchase space so their ads will be seen; therefore all subtle, complex or profound stories must be carefully filtered out even though these might be far more impactful for society as a whole.
News consumption distorts our understanding of the world, leading us to live with an inaccurate representation of risks and threats we actually face.

Second, news is irrelevant. Over the past twelve months, you may have consumed approximately 10,000 news snippets (perhaps up to thirty per day). Be honest: name one that helped you make better decisions in life, career or business when compared with not having this piece of news compared with not having it at all - out of 10,000 stories consumed. No one I asked could name more than two helpful pieces from all that were consumed - a miserable result from news organizations which assert that their information offers competitive advantages when in reality consumption represents an economic disadvantage; had they helped people advance further with career advancement would journalists be at the top of income pyramid - quite the opposite is true

News is also an inefficient use of time: on average, each human wastes half a day each week reading up on current affairs, leading to massive productivity losses worldwide. Take for instance the 2008 Mumbai terror attacks: out of an unquenchable thirst for recognition alone, terrorists killed 200 innocent lives purely to gain fame and recognition. Let's say one billion people spent one hour following the aftermath: viewing minute-by-minute updates and listening to commentaries by experts and analysts - an extremely likely scenario given India has over one billion inhabitants. Therefore, our conservative calculation: one billion people multiplied by an hour's distraction equals one billion hours of work stoppage. If we convert this number to lives lost due to news consumption versus attack losses, this number stands at around 2,000 deaths wasted from consumption alone - an incisive yet precise observation.

Turning away from news can bring equally profound results as purging any of the other ninety-eight bad habits we've outlined here. Break your news habit entirely; read long background articles or books instead - nothing beats books for understanding our world!

See also Fundamental Attribution Error (ch. 36); Sleeper Effect (ch. 70); Confirmation Bias (chs 7-8); Information Bias (ch. 59); Personification (ch 87) and Story Bias (ch 13) as related phenomena.

EPILOGUE

The Pope asked Michelangelo: 'Tell me the secret of your genius. How have you created this statue of David, the masterpiece among all masterpieces?' Michelangelo replied simply by taking away everything that wasn't David.

Let's be clear. No one really knows for certain what makes us successful or happy, yet we do understand what detracts from either success or happiness. Negative knowledge (what not to do) is far more potency than positive knowledge (what should be done).

Michelangelo used Michelangelo's method to think more clearly and act wisely: instead of looking solely at David, concentrate on all that stands in his way and remove them piecemeal; similarly in our case: eliminate errors for improved thinking!

Greek, Roman and medieval thinkers coined a term for this approach called via negativa - literally "negative path", an approach to renunciation, exclusion and reduction. Theologians were early pioneers of via negativa: we cannot say what God is; instead we can only define His absence; applied to modern life: success cannot be defined directly; only what blocks its pursuit can be identified and eliminated - in essence all we need to know!

This hot theory of irrationality bubbled for centuries. John Calvin, founder of strict Protestantism in the 1540s, believed such feelings represented evil and that only by turning towards God could you repel them. People experiencing volcanic eruptions of emotion were considered followers of Satan; therefore torture and killing ensued. According to Austrian psychoanalyst Sigmund Freud's theory, which suggests that our ego and moralistic superego control our impulsive id and suppress it through duty or discipline is something which cannot happen. Forget about obligation or discipline - thinking alone cannot control our emotions to any greater degree than trying to make your hair grow out by willpower alone!

On the other hand, the cold theory of irrationality is still young. After World War II, many attempted to explain away the seemingly irrationality of Nazis - neither emotional outbursts nor fiery speeches were heard from Hitler himself in leadership ranks; even his fiery speeches were just masterful performances - it was cold calculation rather than sudden eruptions that led them down their dark path; same goes for Stalin or Khmer Rouge.

Psychologists began moving away from Freud's claims in the 1960s, and looking scientifically at our thinking, decisions, and actions. What emerged was a cold theory of irrationality which postulated that thinking itself is far from pure; even highly intelligent people fall prey to cognitive traps that lead to errors. Furthermore, errors aren't randomly distributed: errors

tend to cluster into predictable patterns - making mistakes more predictable but never completely fixable - yet their source was unknown for decades - while everything else in our body seemed relatively reliable compared with our brains.
Why must our brains suffer continual setbacks?

Thinking is a biological phenomenon, with evolution having played its part in shaping it just like any other aspect of nature. Imagine going back 50,000 years and taking one of our ancestors back with us into the present - sending him for hairdressing, sending him driving lessons, or teaching him how to operate a cellphone, but no doubt he would fit right in; after all, biological evolution has given us all these abilities as hunters-gatherers that sport Hugo Boss (or H&M in some instances) suits! If we could do just this, imagine going back 50,000 years, taking an ancestor out and bringing him/her/them into present-day time travel; then maybe, instead of being outcast on street, and sending him/her/them from that time into present-day clothing; sending him/her off for haircutting/haircut/dressing at hair salon/dresser/dresses them/them/us to make up in modern dress/clothing? No; Biology has disproved all doubt; physically including cognitively, we are hunters-gatherers dressed in Hugo Boss (or H&M for that matter).

What has changed significantly since ancient times is our living environment. Things were simple and stable back then - people lived in groups of up to fifty people without significant technological or social progress taking place. Only in the last 10,000 years has our world begun to undergo dramatic change, with crops, livestock, villages, cities, global trade and financial markets all emerging as major forces in its evolution. Since industrialisation, much of what was optimal for human brain function has vanished. Spend 15 minutes in any shopping mall, and you will pass more people than our ancestors saw during their entire lifetimes. Anyone claiming they know what the world will look like in 10 years usually becomes an outcast within months after making such predictions. Since 10,000 years, we have created a world that we no longer comprehend. Everything has become more sophisticated yet more intricately connected. As a result, economic prosperity has skyrocketed but also lifestyle diseases (like type two diabetes, lung cancer and depression) and errors in thinking have skyrocketed as complexity has only continued to rise - this will only further compound their errors and magnify them further.

At our hunter-gatherer roots, activity often proved more profitable than reflection. Lightning-fast reactions were essential, while extended contemplations proved fatal. If one of your hunter-gatherer buddies suddenly bolted, it made sense to follow suit; no matter whether a tiger or boar had alarmed you. Failing to run away could cost your life; in contrast if just running from a boar caused error it may cost only calories; being wrong about similar matters paid off: anyone wired differently exited before even encounters occurred - making us all descendants of those homines sapientes who tend towards action being taken quickly by early generations who led. We are their descendants today.

Modern society favors singular contemplation and independent action - anyone who has fallen for stock market hype knows this firsthand.

Evolutionary psychology remains mostly an hypothesis, yet is highly convincing in explaining many flaws; although not all. Take, for instance, this statement: 'Every Hershey bar comes in a brown wrapper; therefore all candy bars that share this characteristic must also be Hershey bars.' Even intelligent individuals can fall victim to this trap - as are native tribes living unencumbered by civilisation - just as our hunter-gatherer ancestors could still experience errors in logic that have nothing to do with environmental change.

Why is that? Evolution doesn't create perfect humans; as long as we advance beyond our competitors (i.e., beat Neanderthals), error-laden behavior is tolerated by evolution. Take the cuckoo bird as an example - for millions of years they have laid eggs in songbird nests where smaller birds then incubated and fed the chicks born from these eggs - an act which represents a behavioral error which evolution has failed to rectify because it wasn't considered serious enough by smaller birds.

An additional explanation for our mistakes emerged in the late 1990s: our brains are wired for reproduction rather than searching for truth; that is, we use our thoughts primarily for persuasion rather than truth-seeking; whoever can convince others gains power and resources - assets which provide a significant edge when mating and rearing offspring. Novels typically outsell nonfiction titles despite their greater candor.

Finally, intuitive decisions - even those devoid of logic - may be beneficial in certain circumstances. So-called heuristic research explores this phenomenon. Since we often lack all of the required information when making important decisions, mental shortcuts or rules of thumb (heuristics) become indispensable. For instance, when choosing romantic partners you are drawn to, the only rational decision would be relying solely on logic; using intuition instead often leads to better results in this case. Many decisions must also be justified later by reasons or justification of some sort - something logic simply cannot.
Decisions (career, life partner and investments) often happen subconsciously. We later formulate justifications so we feel like our choice was conscious, though this often doesn't look anything like scientific methods: instead we make up reasons to justify predetermined conclusions rather than objective facts.

Therefore, forget the dichotomy between left and right brain described by self-help books; much more significant is the distinction between intuitive and rational thinking - both have valid uses; intuitive minds tend to be quicker, spontaneous, and energy saving while rational thought requires much more energy than its intuitive counterpart. Daniel Kahneman famously explained this phenomenon in Thinking Fast and Slow.

People often ask how I manage to lead an error-free life since my cognitive errors began accruing, yet the truth is I don't. And the answer? Nope; not even close. Like everybody else I make snap decisions by consulting not my thoughts but feelings instead; when making decisions quickly the question 'What do I think about this?' is often replaced by "How do I feel about this?" Anticipating and avoiding fallacies is an expensive endeavor;

To keep things straightforward and clear-cut, I have set myself the following rules for decision-making in situations with major potential ramifications (i.e. making key personal or business choices), I attempt to remain as reasonable and rational as possible when choosing between options. My approach is similar to a pilot: I take out my list of errors and check them off one at a time, like an aircraft pilot would do. To help myself make informed decisions more efficiently (i.e. regular or diet Pepsi, sparkling or flat water?), I utilize an excellent checklist decision tree as well. In situations with minimal consequences (i.e. sparkling vs flat water?), the decision tree helps immensely - for instance when choosing between regular versus diet Pepsi or sparkling or flat water). I often forego rational optimisation and let my intuition lead the way instead. Thinking can be tiring; therefore if the potential harm is minimal then don't exert yourself over trivial matters; such errors won't have lasting repercussions and this way of living may bring about better experiences overall. Nature seems unconcerned with whether or not our decisions are perfect; all that matters is that we navigate ourselves through life successfully - as long as we're prepared to act rationally when things get difficult. Additionally, I often rely on my intuition when operating within my circle of competence. Practice an instrument, and your fingers learn to play its notes. Over time, your fingertips become proficient at manipulating keys or strings; musical scores appear and notes play themselves almost automatically - Warren Buffett uses balance sheets like professional musicians do musical scores!
Find your circle of competence - that area in which you intuitively comprehend and excel - and gain a firm grasp. Hint: it may be smaller than you realize! When making consequential decisions outside this circle, apply hard rational thinking techniques while for less pressing decisions use intuition freely.

THE END

The edits and layout of this print version are Copyright © 2023
by I J N

www.ingramcontent.com/pod-product-compliance
Lightning Source LLC
Chambersburg PA
CBHW081911120726

47996CB00010B/3287